Personal Insolvency

Routledge·Cavendish
Taylor & Francis Group

Personal Insolvency

Frank Brumby, Andrew McTear,
Chris Williams & Rosy Border

Routledge·Cavendish
Taylor & Francis Group

First published in Great Britain 2004 by
RoutledgeCavendish
2 Park Square, Milton Park, Abingdon, Oxon, OX14 4RN
Website: www.routledgecavendish.com

Published in the United States by RoutledgeCavendish
270 Madison Ave, New York NY 10016

Published in Australia by RoutledgeCavendish (Australia) Pty Ltd
45 Beach Street, Coogee, NSW 2034, Australia
Website: www.routledgecavendish.com

Transferred to Digital Printing 2006

British Library Cataloguing in Publication Data
Personal insolvency – (Pocket lawyer)
1 Bankruptcy – England 2 Bankruptcy – Wales
I McTear, A
346.4'2078

Library of Congress Cataloguing in Publication Data
Data available

ISBN 1-85941-926-7

1 3 5 7 9 10 8 6 4 2

Printed and bound by CPI Antony Rowe, Eastbourne

Contents

Disclaimer

This book puts *you* in control. This is an excellent thing, but it also makes *you* responsible for using it properly. Few washing machine manufacturers will honour their guarantee if you don't follow their 'instructions for use'. In the same way, we are unable to accept liability for any loss arising from mistakes or misunderstandings on your part. So please take time to read this book carefully.

Although this book points you in the right direction, reading one small book will not make you an expert, and it can certainly never replace the need to take professional advice. This book is not a definitive statement of the law, although we believe it to be accurate as at April 2004.

The authors and publisher cannot accept liability for any advice or material that becomes obsolete due to changes in the law after the publication date, although every effort will be made to show any such changes on the companion website.

About the authors

Frank Brumby is a solicitor, partner and Licensed Insolvency Practioner at Leathes Prior Solicitors. **Andrew McTear** and **Chris Williams** are Chartered Accountants, practising Licensed Insolvency Practioners and partners in East Anglian-based business rescue and insolvency specialists McTear Williams & Wood. All three work closely with people in financial difficulty, or with their advisors, and they see at first hand the issues that most affect individuals in financial difficulties, also known as 'debtors', on a daily basis.

Rosy Border, series editor of the *Pocket Lawyer* series, has worked in publishing, lecturing, journalism and the law. A prolific author and adapter, she stopped counting after 150 titles. She enjoys DIY, entertaining and retail therapy in French markets.

Acknowledgments

A glance at the 'Useful contacts' section will show the many individuals and organisations we consulted while compiling this book. Thank you, everyone. Frank, Andrew and Chris would particularly like to thank David Wood of McTear Williams & Wood, and Sue Sutton of Leathes Prior Solicitors, who provided invaluable suggestions, and long-suffering secretaries Julie and Linda for their support. And Rosy owes a debt of gratitude to her husband, John Rabson, for IT support and coffee.

PERSONAL INSOLVENCY

Welcome

Welcome to *Pocket Lawyer*. Let's face it – the law is a maze. Without a map you are likely to get lost. This book is your map through the part of the maze that deals with personal financial difficulties, the problems of debt in general, and with personal insolvency and bankruptcy – the situation in which you as an individual owe more than you can pay – and the options available to you.

We put *you* in control

This book empowers you. This is a good thing, but control carries responsibility as well as power, so please use this book properly. Read it with care. We have left wide margins for you to make notes. Take your time – do not skip anything:

o   everything is there for a purpose;
o   if anything were unimportant, we would have left it out.

Think of yourself as a driver using a road map. The map tells you the route, but it is up to you to drive carefully along it.

We have done our best to provide accurate and up to date information, but laws and regulations can change. This book is based on the law as at April 2004 and all the useful contacts were accurate on that date.

As with any legal matter, your own common sense will often tell you when you are out of your depth and need expert help. We warn you when you are in danger of getting lost and need to take professional advice. We will alert you to:

o   common traps for the unwary;
o   situations when you are in danger of getting out of your depth and need to take professional advice.

Watch out for the hazard sign.

Sometimes we stop to empower you to do something. Look out for the 'Power point' sign.

Sometimes we pause to explain something: the origin of a word, perhaps, or why a particular piece of legislation was passed. You do not need to know these things to make use of this book, but we hope you find them interesting.

Clear English rules OK

Client to solicitor who has just drafted a contract for him: 'This *can't* be legal – I can understand it!'

Our style is WYSIWYG - what you see is what you get.

Some legal documents have traditionally been written in archaic language, often known as 'law-speak'. This term also extends to the practice of using the names of legal cases as shorthand for legal concepts. This wording has stood the test of time – often several centuries – and has been hallowed by the courts. Some of the words used sound just like everyday language, but beware – it is a kind of specialist shorthand. When we *do* need to use technical language, we offer clear explanations: see 'Buzzwords', p xv. These words appear in the text in **bold** so you can check their meaning.

A note on Scotland and Northern Ireland

This book deals mainly with the situation in England and Wales. While the *general advice* in this book should be helpful to readers everywhere in the UK, the *legal procedures* (court procedure, forms, etc) are different for personal insolvency in Scotland. Although the court forms are different, the *advice* in this book also applies to Northern Ireland.

A note on gender

This book is unisex. We acknowledge that there are both male and female debtors, creditors, insolvency practitioners and so on. We try to allow for this in the text by using, where possible, the generic *they/them* rather than *he/she/him/her*, etc.

Click onto the website

www.cavendishpublishing.com/pocketlawyer

Getting the most from this book

This book sets out the general information the experts would tell you about the subject, if only they had the time and you had the money to pay them. And if you follow our advice you should:

o   recognise when you are in financial difficulty;

o   know what your main options are;

o   make informed choices;

o   having made these choices, understand what the other actors in the drama are likely to do and what happens next;

o   know when you are out of your depth and need to seek professional advice.

Please also bear in mind that the law changes. Not only are new statutes brought into force, and old ones discarded, but the decisions of judges – known as case law or legal authorities – change or are clarified over time, changes which may help or hinder your position.

Case law? Legal authorities? Another term might be 'judge-made' law: *statute law* sets down the rules; *case law* documents the ways in which judges have interpreted those rules in ground-breaking cases known as *precedents*.

One further note: personal insolvency is quite a narrow area and many general advisors (either of a legal or accountancy kind) have little practical experience in providing technical insolvency advice. This is not necessarily a bad thing, but be careful; if you have studied the contents of this book thoroughly you are likely to know as much as the majority of professionals – unless, of course, they have read this book as well!

What this book can do for you

This book:

o provides *general* information and advice about personal debt and insolvency;

o tells you the buzzwords which are important in this section of the law and what they mean;

o answers many of the most frequently asked questions on the subject;

o shows you the key documents and forms that you are likely to come across;

o tells you what each form is for – so that not only do you complete all the paperwork correctly but you also understand what you are doing and why;

o gives you samples of the key letters and other documents you will need before responsibility is handed over to the Official Receiver or an insolvency practitioner;

o offers a 'Useful contacts' section with addresses, telephone numbers and websites;

o is supported by a regularly updated companion website.

What this book can't do for you

This book can't:

o teach you all the ins and outs of personal insolvency law and bankruptcy.

   The leading textbook on bankruptcy alone would make a very good doorstop! We aim for you to be streetwise rather than academic;

o advise in detail on your individual case.

   This book is suitable for *general* advice in straightforward cases, but it is no replacement for the *specific* advice you may need on your individual circumstances;

o make up your mind for you.

   All key decisions require finely balanced judgments. This book puts these into context but it is not a substitute for talking the situation through with a valued friend and then, if appropriate, *getting professional advice*.

Important changes

The Enterprise Act 2002 received Royal Assent on 7 November 2002 and made far-reaching changes to corporate and personal insolvency law. However, when an Act has received royal assent, this does not mean that all the changes it makes are brought into force immediately. The great majority of the personal insolvency provisions did not come into force until 1 April 2004. At the time of going to press, there has not been much case law (see p xi) to help the professionals to interpret the new provisions. This book provides information for those made bankrupt both before and after 1 April 2004.

Buzzwords

As we said before, many trades and professions use special words in the course of their work, or use ordinary words in a different way from those outside their own group. To a chemist and an accountant, *solvent* means two very different things! Eavesdrop on any gathering of doctors, lawyers, plumbers or motor mechanics and you'll see what we mean.

The world of insolvency is no exception. Here are some terms you will find helpful. If we mention in one definition an item which is also defined in this section, we print it in *italics*. In the text, if a buzzword crops up we print it in **bold** to remind you to look it up if you are not sure what it means. We don't do this exhaustively, just when we think you might be glad of a reminder.

administration order – a court order that allows you to make a monthly payment into the court, who will then share out the money among your *creditors* pro rata, ie, according to each creditor's share of your total *debt* (see p 61 for more information).

affidavit – a sworn statement; you swear that what you tell the court is the truth. Affidavits have to be sworn on the Bible (or the Q'ran if you are a Muslim) or affirmed in front of a solicitor or a court official. The alternative is for a witness statement to be signed.

after acquired property/assets – property or other *assets* that a *bankrupt* acquires (by whatever means) during their bankruptcy and before discharge; in many cases, after acquired property and assets will have to be handed over to help pay the *creditors*. Legacies, windfalls and lottery winnings come into this category (see p 118 for more information).

antecedent transactions – there are two main types of antecedent transactions: 'transactions at an undervalue' and 'preferences'. These are deals/transactions which a debtor enters into prior to the date of the bankruptcy order. These transactions can be set aside or reversed by a *Trustee in Bankruptcy* applying to court (see p 115 for more information).

assets – the money and property that belong to you and form part of your total 'worth'; the opposite is **liability**. A £1,000 car that is bought and paid for would be an asset; a £1,000 car with £1,100 worth of finance on it would be a liability.

bailiff – someone who is instructed to act on behalf of a landlord, the tax man, or a *creditor* who has obtained a *county court judgment*. The bailiff has the power to enter your home and take away goods to be sold (see 'A word about bailiffs', p 31).

bankrupt –

o   used as a noun: an individual *debtor* (that is, a person rather than a company) against whom a *bankruptcy order* (see below) has been made by the court;

o   used as a verb: to make a debtor bankrupt.

A bankrupt who has served their time is called a **discharged bankrupt**. One who has not yet done so is called an **undischarged bankrupt**.

To say that companies are 'bankrupt' is not legally correct; only individuals can be made 'bankrupt'. Companies go into liquidation, receivership or administration, which are all different corporate insolvency procedures. If corporate insolvency is your problem, you need *Corporate Insolvency* in the *Pocket Lawyer* series.

bankruptcy order – an order granted by a court which confirms that the *debtor* is unable to pay their debts.

The order also allows the bankrupt's property and other *assets* to be taken away and sold and the proceeds shared among the *creditors*. Unlike the medieval bankrupt (see below), however, a bankrupt is still allowed to earn a modest living.

After a modern bankrupt has served their time there is, unless there has been misconduct or a previous bankruptcy, an automatic *discharge* and, in effect, the bankrupt's slate is wiped clean.

bankruptcy restriction order (BRO) – a court order which has the effect of cramping the style of bankrupts who have misbehaved. The order lasts far longer than the usual bankruptcy period and can remain in force for between two and 15 years, depending upon how outrageously the bankrupt has behaved. This regime came into effect on 1 April 2004 (see p 124 for more information).

In medieval Italy, moneylenders who could not pay their debts were bankrupted. They had their desks or counters – their *bancos* – ruptured or broken by the creditors. A money-lender with no desk was thus put out of business.

---

breach – law-speak for 'break' (a law, a promise, etc); if you do so, you are said to be 'in breach (of section XYZ)' or just 'in breach'.

charge – in this context, a *claim* on property or other *assets*, which has to be met before other *claims* are considered. A mortgage on your home is the commonest form of charge.

claim – in this context, an official form on which a *creditor* tells the court what they want (usually some money you owe) and asks for a judgment in the creditor's favour.

county court judgment (CCJ) – a decision by a court that a *debtor* does indeed owe the money which a *creditor* is claiming from him. A CCJ is a serious matter because CCJs are a matter of public record; even one CCJ will harm your *credit rating*.

credit rating – an estimate of how good a risk you are, based on several criteria (see 'Stay creditworthy!', p 15).

creditor – a person or organisation to whom money is owed.

Credit and *creditor* both come from *credo*, the Latin for 'believe' or 'trust' – as in the Church of England Creed ('I believe in one God ...'). When you buy something on credit, the supplier lets you have it in the belief that you will pay for it. So a creditor is somebody who has supplied you with goods or money in the belief that you'd pay what you owed.

Spotted over the counter of a small grocery store in Tennessee: 'In God we trust; other customers pay cash'.

Crown debt – money that is owed to the Crown (ie, the government; the Queen is unlikely to be involved!). Typically this would be tax (income tax, VAT, etc) or National Insurance.

debt – this is where it gets confusing. The dictionary definition is 'What one owes to another; what one becomes liable to do or suffer; a state of obligation'. In insolvency parlance, *debt* is used to describe an amount due – whether it is owed *by* you (and the claimant is one of your *creditors*) or owed *to* you (and the individual or company is one of your *debtors*). Yes, this even confuses professionals. To get the meaning you have to take the use of the word *debt* in context.

In this book we mostly use this word as meaning 'a sum owed by A (the debtor) to B (the creditor)'.

debtor – and the potential for confusion doesn't stop with the *debt*. The dictionary says a debtor is 'one who owes a debt'. In insolvency circles, *debtor* is used to describe an entity – such as a business or a bank – that owes you money (ie, a customer with an account outstanding) or an individual who owes money to *creditors*, so we would say that the debtor (Mr Smith) is considering going bankrupt. Again, the word can only be understood in context.

In this book we always use this word to mean 'an individual who owes money to creditors'.

default – a failure to keep a promise; the *breach* of a contract.

default notice – a statement (typically from a hire-purchase firm) that you have missed payments on an account, accompanied by a demand for payment. This is a serious matter because, like a *CCJ*, it may harm your *credit rating* (see p 14).

disbursements – expenses; the money a professional, such as a solicitor or a *Licensed Insolvency Practitioner* has to pay out on your behalf. A typical disbursement would be a court fee.

Disbursements is law-speak for 'expenses': money paid out. It comes from old French *bourse*, a purse. And of course a bursar keeps a tight hold on the purse strings and a bursary is an award of money.

discharge – in this context:

o   to release a person, eg, from bankruptcy. A *discharged* bankrupt has served their time. An *undischarged* bankrupt has not;

- o   to remove a court order (such as an administration order or a bankruptcy order) because the conditions have been fulfilled.

distrain – bluntly speaking, to send in the *bailiffs*. The dictionary says 'seize the goods of a debtor'. The noun – the act of distraining – is **distraint** or **distress**.

dividend – when a *Trustee in Bankruptcy* has realised all of the assets and agreed all of the claims of creditors they may have, the Trustee in Bankruptcy then distributes the money to all the creditors. Each creditor receives a 'dividend', ie, for every £1 the creditor is owed, they might receive 25 pence. The dividend is therefore *25 pence in the pound*. This applies similarly to payments made to the creditors by a *Supervisor* of an *IVA*.

Dividend comes from the Latin for 'that which is to be divided'. *Agenda* ('those matters which are to be gone through') comes out of the same stable.

---

enforcement (proceedings) – court action to enforce payment of a debt after a *county court judgment* has been made against the *debtor* (see p 30). Please note that certain *creditors* do not need a county court judgment, principally a landlord, the Inland Revenue or HM Customs & Excise, if they wish to *distrain* on goods.

estate – not your rolling acres or the family Volvo. In this context it means everything you own. Your 'gross estate' is the value of your *assets*, and your 'net estate' is the value of assets less your *liabilities*, ie, any money you owe on them, such as a mortgage on your home or a loan on your car.

extortionate credit transaction – Mafia territory. A deal which gives credit on exorbitant ('12% interest – a week!') or grossly unfair ('Pay in full by Monday, or the boys will break your wrists') terms having regard to the risk accepted by the creditor. A *Trustee in Bankruptcy* can apply to the court asking for such a transaction to be set aside. This will reduce the amount owed to the creditor in the bankruptcy, which may mean that the creditors, as a whole, receive a higher *dividend*.

file/present – take or send a document (eg, a bankruptcy *petition*) to the court.

income payments order – an order from a court for a proportion of a *bankrupt*'s income to be paid to their *Trustee in Bankruptcy*, ultimately for the benefit of the creditors.

When you are made *bankrupt* you are entitled to keep as much of your earnings as is sufficient for what the law calls your 'basic domestic needs'. Any additional income can be subject to an income payments order. When you are made bankrupt the *Trustee in Bankruptcy* will review your income and expenditure and decide what sum, if any, you should pay to the Trustee in Bankruptcy for a period of up to three years. ('Hang on,' you say, 'didn't the Enterprise Act 2002 (see p 49) change this?' No – oddly, it is still three years even if your bankruptcy is discharged after only one year.) In the absence of an agreement between you and the Trustee in Bankruptcy, the Trustee in Bankruptcy will ask the court to make an income payments order. This can be reviewed and amended, either increasing or decreasing your contributions, depending upon how your income changes (see p 102 for more information).

individual voluntary arrangement (IVA) – an agreement for the repayment of *debts* between an individual *debtor* and their *creditors*, supervised by a *Licensed Insolvency Practitioner*. This is a court procedure.

informal arrangement/agreement – an agreement between a *debtor* and their *creditors* without going to court. This is what all the debt agencies advertising on television are offering: no more, no less!

insolvent – unable to pay your debts; owing more than you have. The opposite, of course, is **solvent**. **Insolvency** is the state of being insolvent.

Solvent comes from the Latin *solvere*, which means 'to unfasten, unlock' (like solving a crossword clue) or (in the sense of a debt) 'to pay'. Money is like tap water. It's bad manners to boast about it, and irresponsible to waste it, but when your well dries up you're in deep trouble. It is this drying up that finally does for a debtor, hence the term *insolvent*.

judgment debt – a debt for which a *creditor* has a *county court judgment* (a *CCJ*) in their favour. Having a judgment debt enables the *creditor*, if the money is not immediately forthcoming, to go on to the next stage – *enforcement*.

Licensed Insolvency Practitioner – an individual authorised to act in *insolvency* matters, either by a *recognised professional body* or by a 'relevant authority' such as the Law Society, Institute of Chartered Accountants, the Insolvency Practitioners Association or the DTI. In this book we sometimes abbreviate Licensed Insolvency Practitioner to 'LIP' or 'IP'.

lien – interestingly, *lien* comes from *ligamen*, 'a string'. Something with a lien on it is the opposite of the same thing 'with no strings attached'. A lien *is* a string, in the sense of a right to hang on to goods or property belonging to someone else until debts are paid ('I'll keep your car until you've paid for the repairs'). A lien can also be a form of *charge* over property in favour of a *creditor*, who is allowed to sell that property and use the money to pay the debt.

liquidation – the corporate equivalent of *bankruptcy*. The verb is **to liquidate**. If an individual owes you money you can take *bankruptcy* proceedings. If a limited company owes you money you can take proceedings that lead to liquidation. Therefore, to say that a company is 'bankrupt' is legally wrong, as bankruptcy only applies to individuals.

mitigate – to soften a blow or reduce the severity of something. In the context of an *insolvent* business, an employee with a valid claim can get their wages paid by the government, but they cannot just take the money and run. The employee must *mitigate* that claim by at least claiming unemployment benefit and trying to get another job.

nominee – the person named (nominated) in a proposal to act in the preliminary stages of the implementation of an *individual voluntary arrangement* (see above).

Official Receiver – a civil servant who deals with the administration of *bankruptcies*.

personal service – nothing kinky here; merely the delivery by hand of an important document by leaving it with the recipient (rather than using post, fax, email, etc), because this is what the law requires. Lawyers **serve** documents that ordinary mortals post, fax or deliver by hand. A *statutory demand* requires personal service.

petition – an application to the court (in this context, asking for a debtor to be *bankrupted*). The verb is **to petition** and the person who does it is called the **petitioner**.

preferential debts – picture a queue of people waiting for a bus. Preferential debts are at the head of the queue. These debts must be paid before the unsecured debts at the end of the queue. Preferential debts include employees' wages. After they have been paid, there is often precious little for anyone else.

Proposal – a legal document which sets out for *creditors* the *debtor*'s terms for an *IVA* (see above).

realise – to sell the *assets* of an *insolvent* person or company to raise money to pay the *creditors*.

recognised professional body – well, you wouldn't want a cowboy handling your debt problems, would you? A recognised professional body has the blessing of the Secretary of State. Its members are suitably qualified and licensed to act as *insolvency practitioners* – a safe pair of hands.

security – in this context, something the lender/*creditor* can hold onto in case a *debt* is not paid. A mortgage lender holds your home as security, which is why all advertising for mortgages contains a statement to the effect that your home may be at risk if you do not keep up the payments.

set aside – to throw out a claim or *petition* (as in 'The judge ordered Mr B's petition to be set aside') or to disregard (as in 'The *Trustee in Bankruptcy* set this transaction aside').

statutory demand – a formal demand for payment of a debt, as the first stage of *bankruptcy* proceedings: 'Pay up or else!'.

A statute is a law, and the law lays down the form that this document must take to make it legally binding: nothing else will have the same legal clout. A statutory demand must be made on the official form and *personal service* (see above) on the *debtor* is necessary, except in limited circumstances (see p 87 for an example).

Supervisor – a person appointed to take charge of an *individual voluntary arrangement* approved by the requisite majority of *creditors*.

termination notice – a note that a (typically mail order) firm is closing your account because, they say, you have failed to keep up the payments. They can in fact close your account without notifying you, and it may seriously harm your *credit rating* (see p 14).

Trustee in Bankruptcy (Trustee) – the person who administers and *realises* the *assets* of a *bankrupt* and distributes the proceeds for the benefit of the bankrupt's *creditors*. You can find out more about the Trustee in Bankruptcy on p 99.

unsecured creditor – the poor soul at the back of the queue for payment. This creditor does not hold any *security* (such as bricks and mortar) and will not get any money until the *preferential debts* have been paid. Typically, there is not much left for unsecured creditors, who have no special property rights against the *debtor*.

Frequently asked questions (FAQs)

Here are the questions we get asked most often. All these points are dealt with in greater detail elsewhere in this book but you may find these brief summaries useful.

Personal debt in general

I have seen a TV commercial offering to settle all my debts and leave me with just 'one low, low monthly payment'. Is this too good to be true?

Yes, it is. The internet is crawling with outfits like this too. What this firm is offering is an **informal arrangement/agreement** under another name. They will charge a fee for setting this up (how else could they afford that fancy advertising?) and add that fee to your total burden of debt. This book shows you how to go about getting an informal arrangement for free (see p 56); why pay someone else to do it?

I have been ill and unable to work and I have got myself into financial trouble. What can I do?

Get some free, unbiased advice – your local Citizens Advice Bureau (CAB) or the National Debtline (see 'Useful contacts') would be a good starting point. Their aim is to help you to reduce your repayments to your creditors until you are able to work again. At the same time, they will check that you have been claiming all the benefits you are entitled to. And if you have taken out insurance, now's the time to dig out your policy and make a claim – the CAB can help you with this too (see p 177).

Note that if you are on benefits already, or on a very low income, you may also qualify for free legal advice from any solicitor who takes part in the Legal Services Commission scheme. Look for the LSC logo in their window.

Some debt advice sites are run by the government, by registered charities or by groups of professionals, financed by creditors. We mention several in our 'Useful contacts' section. They do a great job.

But beware! Some of the many supposed debt advice services you will find on the web are in fact commercial organisations hoping to make money out of you and/or your creditors. Key in 'debt advice' and you'll see what we mean.

Check these websites *very* carefully before making contact!

Incidentally, keying in 'personal insolvency' gets you a better class of website, including Leathes Prior, the firm of solicitors in which Frank Brumby, one of the authors of this book, is a partner!

I owe £2,000 on my Passport card. Now Swordfish are offering me six months' free credit if I transfer the debt to them. Is this a good idea?

Yes and no. In the short term yes, because, although you still owe the money, you will not have to pay interest on it for six months, which could give you some useful breathing space while you sort yourself out. But ask yourself:

o Are you likely to pay off the £2,000 in the six-month honeymoon period?

o What is the interest rate after the six months are up?

o What is the interest rate on additional purchases, withdrawals, etc during the honeymoon period?

o Are there any clever elephant traps in the small print?

o Will you be strong-minded enough to cut up your Passport card as soon as you have transferred the balance to Swordfish?

More about this in 'Credit-surfing', p 54.

I have been sent a county court claim for a debt. What should I do?

Act now! If you ignore it, far from going away that county court claim will become a **county court judgment (CCJ)** against you, which will harm your **credit rating** and also add a court fee and interest to the original debt (see p 29 for more information).

I owe someone money and he is turning nasty. Is he allowed to 'send the boys round'?

Depends how the boys behave when they arrive! Seriously though, harassment of debtors is a criminal offence under the Administration of Justice Act 1970. Harassment is not limited to violence or the threat of violence, and it can include threats of publicity and demands which are frequent or aggressive enough to alarm or humiliate the debtor. So shopping you to the *News of the World* would probably constitute harassment, and breaking a few windows certainly would.

Is non-payment of debts a criminal offence?

No, not usually, and it is in fact a criminal offence to try to extract payment by suggesting that it is. *But* if you systematically bounce cheques to obtain goods and/or services or obtain credit knowing full well that you cannot pay it back (or do not intend to), then you may well be committing a criminal offence.

I have been abroad and I have missed three payments on my car. Now the finance company have sent me a Default Notice. What should I do?

Call them up and do some serious explaining. A **default notice** shows up on your credit rating just the same as a **CCJ**. Follow up your phone call with a letter and a cheque – and set up a standing order with your bank for the remainder of the loan period to prevent you from making the same mistake again.

Can creditors take goods back if they're not paid for?

Only in exceptional cases, where

o   your contract of sale says that the goods belong to the seller until they are fully paid for; *and*

o   the goods remain separate from your other property and belongings (so your creditor could take back a TV but not a central heating system); *and*

o   you give the creditor permission to take the goods back (the creditor is not allowed to force entry onto your premises); *or*

o   the creditor obtains a court order to take back the goods.

The garage repaired my car but I can't afford to pay them. Can they hold onto it until I pay up?

The bad news is yes, they can. This is where the garage exercises a **lien** on your car and is allowed to withhold the car from you, for an indefinite period, until payment is made. And if you still don't pay up, the garage owner can ultimately get a court order for the **bailiffs** to sell your car at auction and use the net proceeds towards paying off the debt.

The good news (for you) is that it isn't as simple as that. *The bailiffs* do the selling, *not* your creditor. That is because your creditor does not own the car, so it is not theirs to sell. And of course the car may be subject to a finance arrangement (let's face it, it probably is!), which often means that, whoever sells the car, the finance house will take its money and leave very little for your creditor.

Bankruptcy

Will I go to prison if I am made bankrupt?

Are you kidding, or is there something you haven't told us?

Debtors' prisons were abolished in this country in 1869 (see below) and nobody can send an honest bankrupt to jail. What you *could* conceivably go to prison for is fraud or other dishonesty in connection with your bankruptcy proceedings. There are a number of offences that can be committed if you subsequently become bankrupt. If you really think this may apply to you, for goodness' sake seek professional advice!

Debtors' prisons survived until 1869 and many famous people served time there, including 18th-century author Oliver Goldsmith (whom Doctor Johnson bailed out). Insolvent debtors were required to work within the prison in return for food and lodging.

Debtors with access to money (perhaps through friends or relations) could pay for better conditions. The Debtors' Prison at Lancaster Castle was known as Hansbrow's Hotel, after Captain James Hansbrow, who was Governor from 1833 to 1862. Inmates had all-day visiting rights, the freedom to earn their living, access to newspapers, wine and tobacco, games and concerts, and a weekly market where they could buy fresh food.

Will my bankruptcy be reported in the newspaper?

Yes. It will probably appear in the Public Notices column of your local newspaper among the planning and licensing applications. Bankruptcy notices are not very attention-grabbing (though many professionals have to read them as part of their job) and your case won't hit the headlines unless you are a celebrity (see the sample, p 148).

I am going bankrupt. Will I have to repay all my creditors before I am discharged?

Bankruptcy will free you from your **unsecured** debts. Secured creditors (those who have a legal **charge** – think of a mortgage and you won't be far wrong – or **lien** over something of yours) will keep that **security** even though you are bankrupt. However, your **assets** – with some exceptions (see below) – will be sold and the money used to meet the claims of your **creditors**. If all of your assets have been sold and there is not enough to pay the creditors in full, you will still be discharged. Please note that if you fail to co-operate with the **Official Receiver** or **Trustee in Bankruptcy**, they may apply to court for your discharge to be suspended.

I am a married woman with debt problems. Does my husband become responsible for my debts?

Not for your *personal* debts, but if a debt is in your *joint* names (a common example is the mortgage on your home) then he will be 'jointly and severally liable' for the debt – that is, creditors can pursue him for *the whole of the debt*. And if he (or anyone else) has guaranteed your debts, then whoever *guaranteed* them will remain responsible.

Will I lose my home?

The answer is a definite maybe. If you own an interest (share) in a home or any other property, then any value (known as *equity*) in that property will have to be **realised** for the benefit of your creditors. Suppose you and your partner are buying, with a £40,000 mortgage, a house worth £50,000. The equity – net worth – of the property is therefore £10,000. Your share of the equity is £5,000 and your *creditors* and/or **Trustee in Bankruptcy** will come after you for that £5,000.

A third party, either your partner or a friend, can, however, arrange to buy your share of the property from your **Trustee**. You can find out about this in more detail on p 71.

Can I have a bank account when I am bankrupt?

The good news is yes, legally you can, although you cannot have a big overdraft because you will still be subject to the restrictions on credit that **bankruptcy** imposes (see p 123).

The bad news is that most banks will not accept your application for an account if you are an **undischarged bankrupt**. There are, however, some banks and building societies who will do business with bankrupts – see 'Banking considerations', p 96 for further details.

Will all my possessions be taken away? What can I keep?

You've been reading *The Mill on the Floss*! There is still a misconception that when a person is made bankrupt the **bailiffs** come and clear their homes. This is not the case nowadays. The law allows you to retain the tools, books, vehicles or other equipment that you need to earn a living. You will also be allowed to keep your 'personal and household effects', including furniture, white goods (such as fridges and washing machines) and clothing. This would not, however, extend to 'items of particular value' such as antique furniture and works of art, valuable jewellery, expensive electrical goods (very flashy IT equipment would be fair game) and high-value sporting goods. Jointly-owned items are also fair game – they are sold and the proceeds divided between your **creditors** and the other joint owner. More about this on p 31; see also the advice about dealing with bailiffs, p 32.

Will they take my partner's/children's possessions?

No. But if you have transferred your **assets** to members of your family to avoid losing them to your **creditors** by, for example, giving away your £25,000 Purdey shotgun to your 8-year-old daughter just before going bankrupt, this would be attacked as a 'transaction at an undervalue' (see p 115) and an application would be made to court by the **Trustee in Bankruptcy** to have it **set aside**.

Will I be able to keep my mortgage on?

Yes, provided that:

○   your mortgage lender is confident that you will be able to maintain your regular mortgage payments and deal with any arrears; *and*

○   your **Trustee in Bankruptcy** does not consider that your monthly payments are excessive for your needs when compared with, for instance, the cost of renting a suitable home.

Will I be able to obtain a mortgage or credit once I am discharged from my bankruptcy?

The good news is that it is becoming easier to obtain mortgages and other credit after bankruptcy. We know of one major mortgage provider who will be prepared to consider offering a mortgage on normal interest rates to a bankrupt once they are discharged. There are also several specialist lenders operating in this field, although you will pay a higher rate of interest for several years.

What happens to my pension/endowment/savings?

A **bankrupt's** pension fund is off limits – it is not available to a **Trustee in Bankruptcy** (but see p 119 about excessive pension contributions) unless it is a pension scheme that is not approved by the Inland Revenue or if you were the subject of a bankruptcy petition prior to 29 May 2000. Seek advice if you are not sure! Other savings, such as endowment policies and savings bonds, will go into the kitty to be **realised** in the bankruptcy.

Can I keep my car?

Yes, as long as it is of low value and you can persuade the **Trustee in Bankruptcy** that you need it to get to work. As a general rule, if your car is worth £1,000 to £1,500 it is likely that you will be able to keep it. However, any claim that you need a Range Rover for the school run or a Porsche to get to the golf club will not be acceptable!

Can I run my own business when I am bankrupt?

Yes you can, as long as you:

o   do so in your own name, or the name in which you were made bankrupt; *and*

o   make it clear to everyone you do business with where credit will be given to you of more than £250 that you are bankrupt.

As a sole trader, you will find the financial restrictions of bankruptcy a serious impediment to running a business and, while there is no legal bar as such, the practical problems (such as buying materials when you are only allowed £500 credit – see below) may make it impossible to trade (see 'Bankruptcy cramps your style!', p 123).

I am bankrupt. What happens if I win the lottery or otherwise come into money before I am discharged?

The buzzword here is **after acquired assets** or property. You must inform your **Trustee in Bankruptcy** about any windfalls or inheritances that you receive during your bankruptcy within 21 days of becoming aware of them. The Trustee must then, within 42 days, **serve** notice on you whether or not they wish to claim the after acquired asset. Almost certainly they will.

If you do not inform the Trustee of your windfall you may be held in contempt of court and punished accordingly (prison or a fine). If, as a result of your good fortune, your **creditors** are paid in full with statutory interest (cross that bridge if and when you come to it!), any surplus will be returned to you and your bankruptcy can be annulled.

It is, however, sensible to ask anyone who is likely to mention you in their will to make other arrangements – such as leaving the money to your children instead of to you. This is because anything willed to you during your bankruptcy would go towards paying off your debts, which is unlikely to be what the maker of the will had in mind.

Individual Voluntary Arrangements (IVAs)

I want to enter into an IVA rather than go bankrupt; is it appropriate for me?

It depends on your circumstances. An **IVA** requires the agreement of **creditors** to whom you owe 75% of your total debt (see p 65 for an explanation of this potentially puzzling statement) and as long as your proposal is good enough to attract this level of support, then an IVA is appropriate.

What is the least amount that I will have to pay creditors under an IVA?

Every case is different and there is no specific formula. Your **creditors** will expect your offer to be the best you can make. If your debts are mainly to credit card companies, then they will be looking to receive a minimum of 25 pence in the pound, ie, a quarter of their total debt. Unless you make an attractive offer, they may simply decide to **bankrupt** you and **realise** your **assets** instead.

Will my IVA be reported in the newspaper?

No, there is no requirement for an IVA to be advertised, unlike bankruptcy. There is, however, a central Register of Individual Voluntary Arrangements and this is a matter of public record. Anyone can go into any **Official Receiver's** office, check the record and see you have been in financial difficulties. They can also find a list on the internet.

I want to continue in business – but will my creditors want to do business with me if I have an IVA? How can I overcome their reluctance?

This is always difficult but, provided your suppliers are satisfied that you have done enough to ensure that the continued business is viable, they should be supportive. You are more than likely going to have to trade on a *pro forma*/cash on delivery basis, where you pay up-front for goods and services, at first.

What will happen if I am unable to carry out my proposals?

This will depend upon the terms of your arrangement; but usually **creditors** will insist that a further creditors' meeting is called or that the IVA is failed, which would result in your bankruptcy.

I do not want to include all my creditors in the IVA; can I arrange special deals with some separately?

No, no, *no*! You must provide a full disclosure to your other **creditors** of any that you propose to exclude from the arrangement. Only if you can get the agreement of creditors representing 75% of the total amount owing – not 75% of the number of creditors themselves (see p 65 for a fuller explanation) – are you allowed to deal with some creditors more favourably than others. Furthermore, if there is any evidence to suggest that you have withheld information about a creditor this may be a ground for invalidating your IVA, or worse, a criminal offence!

Will I be able to get credit when I am in an IVA?

It will be difficult and, if credit is available, it will probably be at high rates of interest. The greater the risk, the higher the interest; and you are not a gold-plated risk any more. Lenders will be aware of your status from the various credit reference agencies (see p 11). In any event, it is unlikely that your existing **creditors** would agree to your taking on any significant new credit, other than in the normal course of trade, during the course of an IVA; and this may have to be monitored by your **Supervisor**.

Will I be able to get credit once my IVA is finished?

Yes, most lenders are prepared to grant credit to individuals who have fulfilled their obligations in an IVA. You may, however, have to wait for some time after the conclusion of your IVA before credit facilities are restored. Remember that an IVA is likely to remain on your credit history for six years.

Prevention is better than cure

Keeping debt under control is a bit like keeping yourself healthy. Many otherwise sensible people don't seek professional advice until something starts hurting.

All of us are being offered credit all the time, like children being offered an unlimited supply of sweets. Sweets taste nice at the time, but too many can lead to uncomfortable sessions in the dentist's chair. Credit is the same: it may seem a good idea at the time, but too much at the wrong time can seriously harm your wealth and cause you a lot of stress.

Don't take sweets from strangers

Quite apart from the world of business, where a certain amount of credit is inevitable, society in the 21st century encourages individuals to 'buy now, pay later'. Many people consider it seriously uncool not to have at least one credit card. In some respects they are right, because having a credit card – always provided that payments are properly maintained – can in itself improve your **credit rating** (see p 9).

If you are perceived as a good credit risk, and even if you aren't, you are deluged with junk mail from people eager to lend you money or let you have goods on credit. They may even offer freebies:

'Is the interest rate on your credit card too much? Then don't pay it ... 4.9% APR on Balance Transfers fixed for the life of the balance. No annual fee. Free rucksack.'

Check the small print

However much the credit providers beg you to read them ('IMPORTANT – YOU SHOULD READ THIS CAREFULLY'), the Terms and Conditions are always in murderously small print. Typical Terms and Conditions are set out like this. If you persevere and study the small print of the 'free rucksack' credit card company you will see three snags:

o   The 4.9% APR applies *only to the balance you transfer* from your other card debt. Anything else – purchases, cash withdrawals and so on – carries an interest rate of 1.45% per month, more than 17% Annual Percentage Rate (APR).

o   There is a £1.50 Transaction Charge on every cash withdrawal *in addition to the interest*.

o   'No Annual Fee' is not what it seems. If you transact less than £500 worth of business on your card in 12 months, they will levy an 'Account Servicing Charge' of £15.

There is another elephant trap you may not know about. Assume that you make a purchase on a credit card for £1,000. When you receive the credit card you make a payment towards it but leave a balance. You pay interest not on the balance you leave but *on the whole amount*. So, even if you paid off £999.99, leaving 1p, your next credit card statement will have an interest charge on it as if you owed the sum of £1,000, not 1p!

They didn't put any of that in the body of the ad, did they? The moral is: if you really want a credit card, *choose one that charges a reasonable APR all the time*. Such cards do exist and the internet or the money sections of the newspapers will help you to find them. For example, every Saturday *The Times* 'money section' publishes a league table along with the 'best buys' in everything from mortgages to savings accounts. So do your homework – and if you really want a rucksack, go out and buy one!

PERSONAL INSOLVENCY

You *can* say no

Credit is everywhere. You don't need to go out looking for it; most people get offers through the post (see above) and even over the telephone, sometimes at highly inconvenient moments. This is because the world of financial services is highly competitive. Lenders try to tempt you away from their competitors with attractive-sounding inducements and discounts. If you are wise you will see these 'sweets' for what they are – bribes to lure you astray.

Children are taught at an early age to 'Just say no' to sweets and other blandishments from strangers. Here are a few ways you can say no too.

Credit cards aren't obligatory

Not everyone can resist the temptations of a credit card. We all have weaknesses: Rosy would eat a whole box of Belgian chocolates if she were stupid enough to be in the same room with them. So her home is a chocolate-free zone.

Fortunately, credit cards, like Belgian chocolates, are not compulsory. Of course, a charge card of some kind is very handy for booking flights over the phone or ordering goods on the internet. This is where *debit cards* such as Switch or Delta come into their own. They will do everything your Passport or Swordfish card will do, with one big advantage: debit cards take money straight out of your bank account, and when the cupboard is bare they lock the door. You can't get carried away, at least not once you have reached your overdraft limit.

Credit cards are not always bad news. You may have greater consumer rights if you buy items by credit card. Some credit cards offer quite valuable perks, such as free travel insurance if you pay for your trip by credit card. Another useful extra is purchase protection insurance (remember that TV commercial in which Rowan Atkinson dropped his new binoculars in a lake?).

You are, of course, spoilt for choice but there are websites that help you to select a card to suit you. We liked the Motley Fool website

www.fool.co.uk/cards/howtochoose_tab.htm. Check out also
www.find.co.uk, www.1st-uk-credit-cards.co.uk or www.buy.co.uk
to compare the various goodies offered by credit card companies.

Say no to junk mail

There's a lot of unsolicited mail (the polite term for junk mail) about. You might be invited to switch credit cards, take out a new one or apply for a 'low interest loan' several times a month, but beware! If you take up too many of these offers you could harm your **credit rating**.

This is because credit card companies share information with credit reference agencies (see p 9). If you start applying for several different credit cards, you will set alarm bells ringing: 'Why is this person suddenly applying for so much credit? Is this person a worse credit risk than we thought?' Someone somewhere will make a note of it and you might be refused credit at a time when you really want it.

Junk mail breeds like bacteria: firms sell mailing lists to other firms, so you end up on several lists. Firms mail you because they hope you will buy their wares. But you *can* say no. If you want to avoid being blandished by all that junk mail with its 'exciting opportunities' you can ask the Mailing Preference Service:

Mailing Preference Service
DMA House
70 Margaret St
London W1W 8SS

or call 020 7291 3310

to get your details taken off the mailing lists of every firm registered with them.

Registered? Yes. Reputable direct selling firms are registered with the Mailing Preference Service and take it seriously. You can find out about the MPS from the firms' point of view by visiting the Admar website on www.admar.co.uk/mps.htm

It can take a while for the gush of unwanted mail to slow to a trickle, but you should notice a marked decrease in just a few weeks.

1   It is against the law – the Telecommunications (Data Protection and Privacy) (Direct Marketing) Regulations 1999, no less – for firms that have registered with the MPS to telephone people who have told the MPS they don't wish to receive direct marketing calls. Offenders could even be fined up to £5,000. Contact the MPS; and next time someone calls and offers you yet another 'exciting opportunity' you can ask them if they realise they could be breaking the law.

2   The MPS will keep a record of your request for five years. At the end of that time you will need to register again.

1   The MPS only covers mail addressed to you *personally*. Junk mail addressed to The occupier/homeowner etc won't be affected.

2   The MPS won't stop mail from firms you have previously bought things from, nor will it stop mail from small local firms who routinely mail their clients past and present. If you don't want to hear from them, you will need to call or write to them directly.

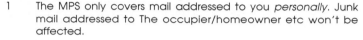

Think twice about store cards

The big stores offer 'sweets' too, such as a discount on their wares as well as several weeks' interest-free credit like an ordinary credit card. Store cards, like other credit cards, don't cause a problem if you pay off the balance within the interest-free period. This is typically between 35 and 55 days. If you fail to do this, however, the interest on the unpaid debt soon mounts up. The 'best' store cards charge 13% APR (Annual Percentage Rate – you'd do better with a bank loan at 8% or so if you were planning a large purchase) and the worst can charge up to a horrifying 30% APR. A government task force is currently looking at store cards and examining whether legislation is needed to control them.

Are 'interest-free' deals a good thing?

Many stores offer so-called interest-free credit on large purchases. Let's suppose you are offered 12 months' interest-free credit on a £600 washer-dryer. Here are the questions to ask yourself:

○ Can you afford to buy the item outright? If so, try haggling for a discount instead of the interest-free credit.

○ Will you be able to pay off this debt within the 12-month period? If the answer is a definite 'yes', you might come out on top. But read the small print carefully, because there is a downside to this apparently generous offer.

If you do not pay every penny back within the six-month period, you may have to pay interest after all – *back-dated to when you took out the agreement.* And the APR could be terrifyingly high. Remember, if you are paying the balance by cheque, the credit provider will require *cleared funds.* Cheques usually take up to five working days to clear and we all know about the Royal Mail! You therefore need to make sure you allow sufficient time for postage and clearance of the cheque, which must be *before* the honeymoon period has expired.

1   The same advice applies here as in 'Credit-surfing', p 54. It boils down to 'Read the small print, keep up the payments and keep good records' (see below).

2   Apart from making sure you clear the debt within the allotted period, you *must* keep good records of all payments, so that you can prove you made the payments at the allotted times. If the lender claims that you missed a payment and you can't prove them wrong, it could either cost you a lot of money in interest charges or start a stressful dispute.

Draw up a budget

Drawing up a budget may not seem the last word in cool chic, but it is the only way we know of looking at your income and your outgoings and seeing how you can – to use a creaking old cliché –cut your coat according to your cloth.

If you have a PC, you can use the spreadsheet facility to do this. Somehow a spreadsheet looks more business-like than hand-written figures on the back of an old envelope, and it is certainly easier to change or add things.

Turn to the Statement of Income and Expenditure (see p 143). This Statement is in fact intended to be sent to **creditors** when you are seeking an **informal arrangement**, but you might like to use it as a starting point for your private budget. If you do so, you may want to break 'Sundry/other expenses' into separate headings, such as:

o   pets;
o   children's pocket money, dinner money and school trips;
o   birthday and Christmas presents;
o   gifts to charity.

Some of these headings may not apply to you, but you can probably think of several more that do.

2

Is your credit good?

Every time you try to borrow money or buy something on credit, someone will check up on you to see if your credit is good. If they think it is, they will accept you as a client. If they are doubtful about you, they will reject you.

Most credit providers – financial institutions, big stores or money lenders – have their own credit scoring or rating system. If you apply for credit they will give you a score based on the information you give them when you apply for the credit.

Credit providers of all kinds also use credit reference agencies. The two best known are Equifax (www.Equifax.co.uk) and Experian (www.experian.co.uk) and you can find their addresses in 'Useful contacts'.

A third agency, Callcredit plc (see 'Useful contacts' for their address and telephone number), is only a couple of years old and is not yet mentioned on all the advice websites, but we liked their website on www.callcredit.plc.uk, particularly the overview of who they are and what they do, and their information on 'blacklisting'.

Credit reference agencies provide potential lenders such as banks, building societies, finance houses and major retailers with information about you. They award you points according to your age, your job, your income, whether you are a homeowner and so on. They also check your credit history (the story of your borrowings and repayments over the years) using many different sources, including the electoral roll and the Register of County Court Judgments (see p 29). It's like a Snakes and Ladders game – you go up a ladder if you own your own home and down a snake if you have a **CCJ** against you.

These agencies do *not* accept or turn down your requests for credit. They simply pass on information to the potential lender, who then uses that information and their own guidelines to decide whether or not to take you on.

Strangely, if you have never had any credit or borrowing then this may not help you – you have no 'experience' of credit. Conversely, if you have had a couple of loans or credit cards, this may increase your credit rating, as you are 'used' to having credit (provided you are not in arrears!).

1   Too much 'experience' of credit could reduce your credit rating.

2   The credit reference agencies will notice if you have had an unusually large number of credit checks carried out – everything from buying a car on interest-free credit to opening a new credit card leaves a sort of electronic Post-It in your file.

Note: blacklists are a myth!

Many people believe that they, or the addresses where they live, can be put on a 'blacklist' of bad credit risks. The credit reference agencies themselves go out of their way to explode this myth on their websites. They insist that:

○   they do not hold a 'blacklist' of individuals; and

○   people who have lived in your home before you do not affect:

    – you,

    – your credit score, or

    – your credit rating.

They will show up on the computer as previous occupants, but this does not imply that they are connected with you financially or in any other way and they do not affect your credit rating.

Check your own credit file

Under section 7 of the Data Protection Act 1998 you are entitled to apply for a copy of your credit file; and Experian alone receives a million requests every year. The current fee is £2 per application. You can apply:

o   *online* – key in the agency's website address (see p 9), access their online form and follow the instructions. You will need a credit or debit card to pay.

o   *by post* – you must give the following details:

  –   full name (including title)
  –   any other name you are known by (eg, maiden name)
  –   your date of birth
  –   your full current address including house number/name, district, post town and postcode
  –   any previous addresses you have lived at during the last six years. List each address separately including house number/name, district, post town and postcode.

Send with a cheque for £2 made payable to

Equifax plc at

Equifax plc
Credit File Advice Centre
PO Box 1140
Bradford
BD1 5US

Callcredit plc at

Callcredit plc
PO Box 491
Leeds
LS3 1WZ

or

Experian Ltd at

Experian Ltd
Consumer Help
PO Box 8000
Nottingham
NG1 5GX

Note that all the agencies hold data on partnerships and sole traders too. Information is held under the name you trade under. Otherwise the procedure for applying for your file is the same.

You should receive your credit rating in seven days together with a helpful leaflet. It is worthwhile undertaking a search against all of the above as certain financial institutions 'subscribe' to some agencies and not others.

You don't need to be applying for credit to ask to see your file. You can do this at any time. And if anything on it is wrong you have the right to correct it. Read on!

Repairing your credit rating

Suppose, when your credit file arrives, it is not (pardon our play on words) a credit to you. You may be able to 'repair' your **credit rating**. But beware of companies that offer to do it for you for a fee. *If your credit rating can be repaired, you can do it yourself free of charge.*

Major credit reference agency Experian (www.experian.co.uk) in particular issues a warning about credit repair companies. They point out that many of these companies make completely false claims about what they can do for you.

Experian advise you to deal directly with them instead. If they feel you would benefit from debt counselling, they will refer you to a free provider such as the Citizens Advice Bureau (CAB), the Consumer Credit Counselling Service, or a solicitor offering a free diagnostic interview. They will help you to correct any wrong information, and also to add brief statements to your file explaining the circumstances that led to any financial problems that show up on your file.

At the time of writing, Experian is involved with a working party to protect consumers from bogus credit repair companies, and also pressing the Office of Fair Trading and the Department of Trade and Industry to take action against what they call 'the more unscrupulous of the credit repair companies'. Additionally, they have asked the Lord Chancellor to 'review current legislation in view of the successful Federal law which protects consumers from being charged up-front by credit repair companies in North America'.

There is, of course, a limit to how much you – or anyone else – can do to repair your credit rating if it contains unfavourable information.

Fraud!

Some credit repair firms issue booklets professing to show you how to make successful applications for credit. They explain the credit scoring system and tell you what to say in order to score highly. What they *don't* say is that giving false information on a credit application form could amount to fraud – a serious criminal offence. Will the police come after the credit repair firm that put you up to it? Well, what do *you* think?

DIY credit repair

Instead of paying a credit repair firm for dodgy advice, get sound advice free, either from sites such as the Insolvency Helpline www.insolvencyhelpline.co.uk (see below) or from the credit reference agencies' own consumer help services.

The Experian site directs you to www.ukcreditrepair.co.uk which lists several useful contacts (all of which you will find in 'Useful contacts'), and also gives details of a booklet called *No Credit?* from the Information Commissioner. Just call 0870 4421211 and ask for your free copy.

CCJs: typically, credit repair firms will claim to be able to remove CCJs from your record, and offer advice about it. To get it, you often have to call a premium rate number for more information. Guess who pays for the call, and guess who gets most of the money!

The fact is that a CCJ, once it is on your record, stays there unless it has been discharged, or was wrong in the first place. Just saying that you never received the claim, or that the correct procedure was not followed, will not take the CCJ off your file. Which leads on to:

Default notices cannot be removed from your record without the agreement of the finance company. Fortunately, the Insolvency Helpline www.insolvencyhelpline.co.uk/default-notices/how-to-remove-default-notices.htm tells you how to go about getting default notices and **termination notices** removed from your credit record. We repeat their advice in case you do not have access to the internet:

o   You can remove a default notice if:

–   the notice was served but the payments have been brought up to date; *or*

–   you are still behind with the payments but you have come to an arrangement with the finance company; *or*

–   you disagree with the default notice being sent in the first place (in which case you will need to explain why).

In any of those cases you need to:

o   write to the lenders and ask if they are willing to remove the notice from your file;

o   if they agree, ask them to put it in writing. They may want an administration fee for this;

o   write, enclosing a copy of the lenders' letter, to the credit reference agencies (addresses in 'Useful contacts') and ask them to remove the notice from your file.

Just to check, write to the credit reference agencies after a few weeks enclosing £2 and asking to see your file.

---

o   To remove a termination notice:

–   write to the mail order company with the account details and ask them for the balance on your account, and whether they agree to the removal of the termination notice from your file if you bring the account up to date.

–   The lenders should then write back with the balance, and either agree to your request or suggest a different solution.

–   Once you are agreed, send the lenders the money and ask them to write to you confirming that they are prepared to have the notice removed from your file.

– When you receive their confirmation, write to the credit reference agencies enclosing a copy and asking them to amend their records.

Again, just to check, write to the credit reference agencies after a few weeks enclosing £2 and asking to see your file.

'Associations'

The credit reference agencies also keep a record of any other person with whom you may have an association, in particular if you have applied for a joint loan/bank account/mortgage. If for any reason you split up from that person, your previous connection with them will stay on the file. This may cause a problem if that person then develops a bad credit rating, as this may have an impact on you. As long as you have no outstanding joint accounts, loans, etc, you can file a Notice of Non-Association which will remove their details from your credit file.

Equifax/Experian normally provide a draft Notice for you sign; alternatively you can send a simple letter to the lenders confirming that you do not wish to be associated.

Stay creditworthy!

Here are some tips to help you stay creditworthy.

Make payments on time. Late or missed payments could stay on your file for up to six years. If a hiccup in your payment record was your lender's mistake, or if you made a genuine mistake and then put the matter right ask them to make sure that it will not affect any information about you that they send to a credit reference agency.

Get on the Roll. If you move house, ask the local authority to send you the forms to put you on the Electoral Roll as soon as possible. Credit reference agencies use Electoral Rolls to check your identity and your address.

Tell your lenders before you move house. Give them your new address in good time. Not only will it help with credit reference checks (by proving that you live where you say you do), it could also forestall fraud by someone opening your mail at your old address and using the information for criminal purposes.

Foil identity fraud. If important papers such as your driver's licence or passport are lost or stolen, as well as telling the police you should also apply for protective registration with CIFAS, the Fraud Prevention Service, in case someone tries to use your documents to obtain credit. The scheme is administered by Equifax (see above), who will put a note on your credit file with all the credit reference agencies.

A year on the Register costs £11.75. You can call the Protective Registration Team on 08700 102 091 and pay by credit card over the telephone. They will need the following details:

o   full name;

o   date of birth;

o   full address with postcode;

o   the names of anyone else living at the address, and their date of birth;

o   home and work telephone numbers;

o   a crime reference number if applicable;

o   details of why you need Protective Registration (eg, lost driver's licence),

and you will receive confirmation by post.

Alternatively, you can send the same details and a cheque for £11.75 made payable to Equifax Ltd to:

CIFAS
PO Box 1141
Bradford
BD1 5UR

They will enter the information on your file with all the credit reference agencies, where it will stay for one year unless you apply to extend or remove it, warning credit providers of a possible fraud.

If you are turned down for credit, ask why. If the information that damned you came from a credit reference agency, ask which one; then apply to see your file (see above). Ask for your file regularly – a lot can happen in a year.

If you find wrong information on your file, put it right (see above).

For example, if your credit file contains information about another member of your family, and you have no financial connection with them, write to the credit reference agency and explain this.

3

Credit – the downside

Very few people can live completely without credit nowadays. Even fanatical adherents to the 'Neither a borrower nor a lender be' philosophy (note for anoraks: this comes from a father's advice to his son in Shakespeare's *Hamlet*; and the next line is 'For loan oft loses both itself and friend') probably have mortgages on their homes. A mortgage is probably the biggest **debt** you will ever incur; but it doesn't pose any threat as long as you keep up the payments.

Most people buy electricity, gas and water on three months' free credit. Every quarter someone reads the meter and the supplier bills us for what we have used. Provided we pay the bills we can continue buying utilities on credit indefinitely, because the providers know we can be trusted.

Credit comes from *credo*, the Latin for 'believe' or 'trust'. When you buy something on credit, the seller lets you have it in the belief that you will pay for it. **Debt** comes from the Latin word for *owe*. So when you buy something on credit but fail to pay, make no bones about it: you are in debt.

Other people use credit to buy large items, such as cars or home improvements. Some firms offer very good deals at low interest rates and you can do well as long as you keep up the payments that you have agreed to make. The same goes for any other borrowings – don't overstretch yourself, keep up the payments and everything's fine.

But what happens if something goes wrong and you *can't* keep up the payments? You are in debt. People can get into debt (call it financial difficulties if it makes you feel better) for all sorts of reasons. Common ones include:

- o unemployment;
- o sickness or injury;
- o bereavement;
- o marriage breakdown;
- o living beyond their means.

Payment protection insurance can soften the blow. Many firms offer it – you have only to key in 'payment protection insurance' on the web to be deluged with offers. It's no use taking it out when you are already having problems, however.

You may have payment protection insurance already without realising it. Many lenders insist on your buying it when you take out the loan, and add the premium to the amount you owe. Check the small print of your loan agreements to see if you are covered, and if so, what your entitlements are.

Is this you?

Running out of money before the end of the month

If life is otherwise fairly normal – no major upheavals, just some month left at the end of your money rather than the reverse – take a cold hard look at your income and outgoings and try to work out why this is happening:

- o Where is your money going each month?
- o Why are you overspending?
- o Is this a temporary blip or is it likely to continue?
- o Can you make savings anywhere?

If you can sort things at this stage, well and good – but keep an eye on your income and outgoings; financial anxiety could be just a car repair bill away.

If you think you are running into difficulties, go to 'Communicate!' below.

Reduced income or increased expenses due to unemployment

There's a lot of it about. You will, of course, be looking for work.

Remember also that you may qualify for benefits. Do not feel ashamed: you have paid tax and National Insurance contributions and you must claim your entitlements. Call a Citizens Advice Bureau or the Benefits Agency (both in your local telephone directory).

Are you insured? We mentioned payment protection insurance. Additionally, many people take out insurance against being unable to work because of illness, accident, etc. Are you one of them? In all the anxiety and upheaval it may have slipped your mind – dig out your policy and prepare to make a claim.

Meanwhile, go to 'Communicate!' below. Creditors are usually quite sympathetic if you let them know what is happening, less so if you don't. So keep them in the picture.

Reduced income or increased expenses due to family break-up

Splitting up should carry a wealth warning. Unless your other half has left you very nicely off indeed, go to 'Communicate!' below. As before, most creditors are sympathetic if you let them know what is happening, less so if you don't keep them in the picture.

Meanwhile, seek professional advice to make sure that, among other things:

o   you (and that includes any children) receive everything you are entitled to from your partner; and

o   you are not saddled with debts that are not your responsibility.

You might qualify for benefits and, in any case, there is a wealth of free advice, starting at your local Citizens Advice Bureau and Benefits Agency (you will find their details in your telephone directory).

Financial difficulties due to bereavement

When there is a death in the family there can be a lot of bills to be paid straight away, together with long delays in releasing any money that is coming to you. As before, always tell your creditors what is happening – see 'Communicate!' below. And check whether there is any relevant insurance in place.

Financial difficulties due to ill health or injury

Ill health is always distressing. It can be particularly hard on self-employed people, and most lenders know all about this. Go to 'Communicate!' below and let them know what is happening.

Remember also that you may qualify for benefits. Your first port of call should be your local Benefits Agency (in the telephone directory under 'Benefits'). Turn to 'Useful contacts' for helpful websites.

Check also any insurances you may have.

Communicate!

You don't have to leave a bill unpaid for long before the red reminders, warning letters, **default notices** and even unpleasant telephone calls start arriving. You may be tempted to ignore them in the hope that they'll go away. They won't.

All the experts will give you the same advice in this situation:

o   Face facts.
o   Open mail and answer the telephone.
o   Tell your creditors what is happening.
o   Always tell the truth.
o   Keep a copy of every letter you send and make a note of every telephone conversation, including the date, what was said and the name of the person you spoke to.

Good record-keeping is vital. You may think you'll remember what was said, but we guarantee that in a week's time your memory will be as hazy as anyone else's. On-the-spot notes, which professionals call file notes or attendance notes, are an invaluable record.

First things first

You don't want to be left homeless or without light, heat or water, or to face criminal charges. Here are the debts you should tackle first:

○ *Mortgage or rent arrears*

When your mortgage lenders say your home may be at risk unless you keep up the payments, they mean it! But they can be sympathetic and helpful if you are honest with them.

○ *Utilities – electricity, gas, water*

Utility companies can and do cut off supplies for non-payment. In a worst-case scenario you could find yourself without light, heat or water.

○ Utility companies can cut off supplies, but they don't usually pursue persistent non-payers themselves. Typically they pass the file to huge **debt** recovery companies who have a tried and tested recovery procedure: threatening letters, Notice of Court Proceedings, the lot. These firms are very difficult to stop once they get going.

So *contact the utility company as soon as the first reminder arrives* and before your case can be handed to the debt collectors. Explain what is happening and ask for time to pay. Keep a file note of the conversation.

○ Consider asking for your electricity or gas to be put on a prepayment meter until you have cleared your arrears. The supplier may be able to set the meter to charge more for the power you use until your arrears are cleared.

This an expensive way of buying power, but it means you can pay as you go and you can't run up a big bill again.

○ *Council tax arrears*

Just before the beginning of each financial year (usually the end of March), an individual or business will receive a notice from the local authority/council confirming the business or council rates due for the following year, ie, April until the following March. There are two options: either pay the sum in full or elect to pay by way of 10 instalments under the statutory instalment scheme. If one of the instalments is not paid on time, the procedure is as follows:

–   the local authority may make a demand for payment of the outstanding instalment;

–   if payment is not made within the required period, a further demand is made giving seven days to pay the outstanding instalment;

–   if payment is still not made, the individual or business loses the right to pay by instalments and must pay the entire balance due for the rest of that year;

–   if the balance is not paid, the local authority can apply to the local magistrates' court for a 'liability order' which then gives the local authority the ability to take any of the **enforcement proceedings** set out on p 30.

Note: the local authority also have the power to apply for you to be sent to prison if business rates are not paid, although this is rarely done. For those with an eye for detail, and the desire to perform research, the relevant legislation is the Council Tax (Administration and Enforcement) Regulations 1992.

o   *Child Support/maintenance*

These are linked with family break-up and will normally involve the courts and/or the Child Support Agency. Both can be fairly vicious and you may wish to seek expert advice from a family lawyer.

o   *Fines*

Even a speeding ticket could eventually land you in prison if you ignore it!

Credit card debts come lower down the list of priorities, because the providers can't cut off your water supply or make you homeless. But they *can* cut off your credit, and the same rules apply: you *must* communicate.

Finally, remember these three DO's when dealing with creditors:

o   Answer letters and phone calls.

o   Tell them what's going on.

o   Keep good records (see above).

And, just as importantly, remember these four DON'T's:

o   Don't borrow more money to pay off your debts without taking professional advice.

o   Don't borrow money to meet interest payments on a debt.

o   Don't sell goods which you still owe money on without repaying the finance company out of the proceeds – you could be committing a criminal offence.

o   Don't use the good creditworthiness of your family or friends to borrow more.

Now read on.

.

County court judgments – and making them stick

Debtors may end up with **county court judgments (CCJs)** against them. A CCJ opens the door to **enforcement proceedings** (see below), but creditors may try other tactics before they resort to court proceedings – **default notices** and **termination notices**, for example. Now read on.

Default notices

To **default** is to go back on a promise, or to be in **breach** of a contract. Banks, building societies or hire purchase firms may send you a **default notice** if you fail to keep up your payments. Default notices affect your **credit rating**.

They have the right to do this to you. When you take out a loan or sign a hire purchase agreement you sign a declaration that, if you fail to keep up the payments in any way, you agree that the lender has the right to tell the credit reference agencies about this.

Firms that are governed by the Consumer Credit Act 1974 have to issue a default notice before they can start any legal action. The next stage may be a county court claim (see below).

Don't delay – act today

As we said, a default notice shows up on your credit record, so you need to deal with it before the lender tells the credit reference agencies. Call the lender as soon as possible. If you can pay off your arrears at once, and then keep up your payments, you should promise to do so and send a cheque for the arrears at once. If not, work out how much you can pay on account and offer this, following up your call in writing.

Prompt action is vital, because unless you can clear up the matter your lender will inform the credit reference agencies and the default will go on your record and harm your credit rating.

If your default notice is just one of several unpleasant communications from creditors, turn to '**Informal arrangement**', p 56.

Termination notices

A termination notice usually arises from a mail order account. You have bought a lot of stuff from a Global, Apex or Tinywoods catalogue and have fallen behind with your payments.

Typically, mail order companies do not send out reminders to their customers. After you have missed a few payments they may hand your file over to a debt recovery firm. Or they may simply close your account and send a termination notice to the **credit reference agencies**, who will put it on your record, thus harming your **credit rating**. They don't usually notify you about this, however. The moral is, of course, not to neglect payments to mail order firms just because they don't pester for payment. They will simply terminate your account and tell their friends (ie, the credit reference agencies) that you are a bad credit risk.

County court claims

A county court **claim** is the final step before a **county court judgment (CCJ)** for debt. Typically you would receive a reminder about your debt, then a final warning which ends like this:

'I must ask you to settle this bill within the next seven days. If you fail to do so, I shall take legal action against you without further warning to recover the debt together with interest and costs. You should note that county court judgments are registered and may make it difficult for you to obtain credit in the future.'

They are correct on both counts.

You can read more about such letters from the creditor's point of view in *Debt Recovery* in the *Pocket Lawyer* series.

One sentence crops up again and again in advertisements in the newspapers offering loans to people with less than perfect credit ratings: '**CCJs**? No problem.'

It may not be a problem for them, but it is for you. Once you have a CCJ against you it goes onto the Register of County Court Judgments which anyone can access for a small fee (see 'Useful Contacts' for details). Any money a firm lends you after a CCJ will therefore be at a higher interest rate because of the increased risk that you will once again fail to pay up. And a CCJ does your **credit rating** (see Chapter 2) no good at all.

The next thing you will receive, if you resolutely ignore all the warnings, is a document with the court's seal on it and a hearing date (the date on which your case comes up). This is a county court **claim**. A claim is bad news, not only because it will affect your creditworthiness if the judge finds against you, but because the fee that the creditor has paid to the court for dealing with their claim is added to your original debt.

Until recently, this document was called a summons (because it summoned you to appear in court) and your **creditor**, who is now called the *claimant*, was known as the *plaintiff* (from the old French word *plainte*, a complaint). The names were changed as part of recent moves to make the law more understandable to non-lawyers. But, whatever you call it, this document is not a thing to be ignored.

Every claim comes with explanatory notes telling you what to do next. If these notes are less than crystal clear to you, seek advice (see 'Useful contacts'). If you live within easy reach of a county court, consider asking one of the clerks there to help you. They deal with such things every day.

There is just one set of circumstances in which a **CCJ** *can* be good news. You must have a CCJ against you on order to qualify for an **administration order** (see p 61).

Enforcement proceedings

The trouble with a CCJ is that it can open the door to **enforcement proceedings** – bad news if you have any **assets**. Orders the judge can make to enforce a judgment include:

○ *attachment of earnings order* – a court order for your employer to pay your creditor a monthly sum out of your earnings;

○ *garnishee order* (now called a 'third party debt order') – a court order for a debtor's money in a bank or building society account to be paid direct to a claimant to pay a **judgment debt**;

○ *charging order* – a court order by which a judgment debt is secured against the debtor's home or other bricks and mortar.

Think of a charging order as a type of mortgage with your creditor in the position of the mortgage lender, although they will not get paid by instalments. They will have to wait until the property is sold, although they can force the sale of your home. Creditors can also get a charging order on investment **assets** such as shares;

○ *warrant of execution* – not an appointment with the headsman but an authority given by the court for the **bailiffs** to swing into action. The warrant allows the bailiffs to enter the debtor's home or business premises and either collect money to pay a debt or take away the debtor's belongings to sell at auction (see below).

A word about bailiffs

A **bailiff** is someone who is:

o   acting on behalf of a **creditor**;

o   enforcing a fine;

o   acting for a landlord to carry out an eviction;

o   acting for a creditor to repossess goods on which you owe money;

o   enforcing a court order such as a **CCJ**.

Note that, while other creditors need a judgment first, then a warrant of execution (see above) to send in the bailiffs, three other creditors can go ahead without a judgment. These are landlords, HM Customs & Excise and the Inland Revenue. None of these needs either a judgment or a warrant of execution before unleashing the bailiffs. A local authority, when pursuing unpaid business or council rates, does not need a judgment either, but they *will* need a liability order granted by the magistrates' court.

When is a bailiff not a bailiff? When he's a sheriff. If you have a judgment against you in the High Court in London, a sheriff rather than a bailiff will call. Neither can do so without a warrant of execution. Medieval, isn't it?

Bailiffs' powers

A bailiff has the legal authority to enter your home and take away goods which will be sold – usually at auction – to repay the money you owe. This is called **distraint**. There are court bailiffs or sheriffs, and there are private firms of bailiffs, and they can all seize your goods to pay:

o   rent arrears;

o   council tax or poll tax arrears;

o   other unpaid taxes;

o   magistrates' court fines;

o   county court judgment debts.

Since 1998 all **bailiffs** have had to be 'certificated': they have a licence from the court allowing them to act as bailiffs. If a bailiff calls on you, check that they are certificated. They must show you written authorisation and follow certain procedures.

Assuming they *are* certificated, bailiffs have powers as follows:

o They can call at your house at any reasonable time to seize goods.

o They are not allowed to break into your home by force, but they can legally enter your property 'peacefully' (the law's word, not ours) through open windows or unlocked doors.

Don't sign anything. Bailiffs sometimes leave papers for you to sign or post them through the letterbox. You don't have to sign anything and you should not even consider doing so until you have called an expert – try your local Citizens Advice Bureau or the National Debtline (0808 808 4000) – for advice or, if you have access to the internet, go to www.nationaldebtline.co.uk.

Don't let them in. You don't have to. Some bailiffs will try to trick their way into your home, saying they only want to use your telephone or your loo. Be like the Three Little Pigs and *lock all your doors and windows*, because:

o If once you do let them in, or if they have managed to enter 'peacefully', such as through an open window, they are allowed to call again and enter forcefully – this time even without your permission – and seize your belongings.

o Once inside, they are allowed to go into every room in your home and can force their way into other parts of your property.

o For example, they can force their way into separate buildings such as sheds and garages regardless of whether you let them into your house itself.

o They can seize goods that are not actually in your home, such as items at your workplace or in a friend's house, or cars or motorbikes parked outside.

What the bailiffs can't touch

There are some things the bailiffs are not allowed to take. By and large, the rules are the same as in Chapter 13. In general, they cannot seize the following items (but see also the 'Hazard signs' below):

o   clothing, bedding, furniture, household equipment or other 'basic domestic needs';

o   tools, books, vehicles or other equipment that you need to earn a living.

But:

o   **Bailiffs** acting in connection with council tax, VAT and income tax may have the right to do so.

o   While a van with your name on the side would normally be exempt, your high performance sports car would not. Also:

– goods which are not yours, such as your son's electronic keyboard;

– goods which are subject to a hire purchase agreement.

But they *can* seize goods you own jointly with someone else, in which case they have to give half the proceeds of sale to the other owner.

Bailiffs are not allowed to:

o   force entry into your home;

o   leave the premises in an unsafe condition when they go;

o   threaten you;

o   use offensive language.

A **bailiff** might threaten to have you sent to prison for not co-operating. This is an empty threat. Bailiffs have many powers, but this is not one of them.

Note that entering 'peacefully' can include shinning over garden walls and coming in through unlocked doors and open windows – see above. And once they have entered 'peacefully' the bailiffs have the right to force entry next time and take away your goods.

'Walking Possession' agreements

When we say the bailiffs seize your goods, this does not mean that they take them away at once. Instead, they will make a list of the items to be taken. Once the bailiffs have identified goods in this way you have a duty to take good care of them and not remove them from your property. This has the odd name of 'Walking Possession'.

The origin of 'Walking Possession' seems lost in the mists of time. Frank's guess is that the bailiff 'walked in and took possession' of goods, and this has been shortened to 'walking possession'.

What can you do?

You will never receive a call from a bailiff out of the blue. You will know you owe money, and you should at least receive a letter saying that unless you pay up in a certain time a bailiff will call. The same letter will normally give you a contact number. Call that number and ask to arrange to pay as much as you can afford straight away. If the answer is yes, it will save you both trouble and money. Trouble? Well, that's obvious. But money too, because bailiffs actually charge *you* for calling at your home and seizing your goods.

If you do receive some warning of a visit from the bailiffs, you could leave your possessions with friends, or hide them in your home – although they are allowed to search for them once they have got inside, and they tend to know all the good hiding places.

o   You must not hide anything that is already on the bailiffs' list (see Walking Possession agreement, above). If you do, you will be committing an offence. If you remove or hide assets to protect them from the bailiffs, you are committing an offence called poundbreach (another mysterious term). Further, if you are made bankrupt and have committed poundbreach, it is a criminal offence.

o   If you are concerned about a bailiff's behaviour, you can complain to their masters. But do get advice first, because the law on this subject is very complex. Call your local Citizens Advice Bureau or the National Debtline (see 'Useful contacts').

5

Personal insolvency – symptoms and strategies

Up to this point we have concentrated on helping you to keep afloat. The next section of this book assumes you are floundering. Personal **insolvency** is a real possibility.

What is personal insolvency?

Well, *insolvency* means being unable to pay your **debts** and *personal* means it affects you as an individual. The equivalent for a limited company is, of course, *corporate insolvency*. Personal insolvency applies not only to the individual with credit card debts, but also to:

○ a sole trader running a business; and

○ a partnership in business.

Even if a debt is a business debt, if you are a sole trader or a partner, you are personally *liable for it.*

There is a different regime for limited companies that become insolvent, which is dealt with in *Corporate Insolvency* in the *Pocket Lawyer* series.

Are you insolvent?

There are two questions to ask.

Are your total liabilities greater then the value of your assets?

In other words, do you owe more than you own? If the answer is yes, then you are, strictly speaking, **insolvent**. However, this test is not always appropriate as it is unlikely that all of your personal debts will be called in at the same time. Most people would faint if they received a demand for their entire debt to their mortgage lender to be paid in seven days, or else! This is known as the 'balance sheet test' for insolvency and is explained in more detail in Chapter 6.

Can you pay your debts, 'as and when they fall due'?

This is the more common test. For example, if you have certain monthly payment commitments (such as mortgage repayments, hire purchase or credit card debts) and you can pay them all each month, then you are *not* insolvent, however heavy your total burden of debt may be, because *the whole amount that you owe is not all due at once*. If, however, you cannot maintain your monthly repayments as well as your other financial commitments (such as food and utilities), then this is the first sign that you are personally insolvent. This is known as the 'cashflow test' for insolvency and is explained in more detail in Chapter 6.

The warning signs

Whether you are an individual unable to pay your credit card bills or a sole trader unable to meet your weekly payroll, financial difficulties and ultimately insolvency show up in the same way: *you run out of cash*. If you type 'insolvency' on your PC, then use the thesaurus facility, you will be offered 'bankruptcy', 'liquidation', 'ruin' and 'collapse', which sums it up nicely.

Relatively few people go bust overnight, however. There are usually warning signs. If you take notice of these signs and act on them at an early stage you may never become insolvent. It is a bit like toothache really: many sufferers put off going to the dentist until the pain is unbearable. Regular checkups and the occasional filling would have saved a lot of grief.

'Annual income twenty pounds, annual expenditure nineteen nineteen six, result happiness. Annual income twenty pounds, annual expenditure twenty pounds ought and six, result misery.' (Mr Micawber in *David Copperfield*)

Mr Micawber was drawn from life. Mr Dickens senior was imprisoned for debt and 12-year-old Charles had to leave school and go to work in a factory. There was, however, a happy ending to this sad tale: the family fortunes improved. Charles completed his education and became a great novelist.

They say the spectator sees more of the game. This is true in insolvency. The warning signs are more obvious to a casual observer than they will be to you. When you are in the thick of it, punch drunk from fending off creditors and juggling your budget, what an outsider would see as a big problem may appear quite normal to you. Pressure from **creditors** usually builds up gradually over several months, possibly even years, and therefore it can be genuinely difficult to see when you have crossed the line from honestly prioritising your financial affairs to recklessly borrowing more money with no realistic prospect of being able to pay it back.

There is no definitive answer to this – and if you are in doubt you should seek independent professional advice – but look at 'Traffic lights', below. If you are experiencing any of these problems, you may be either insolvent already or hurtling towards insolvency.

Traffic lights

 Go ahead but keep under review

o   You are unable to pay **creditors** in accordance with normal terms, but they appear to be happy to continue providing credit and services to you subject to interest charges and late payment penalties.

- You are unable to pay arrears to the tax man on time, but you are able to pay current tax and have agreed a payment schedule to repay the arrears.
- You are on stop because you have exceeded your current credit limit (although you are paying on agreed terms), but you are able to get credit elsewhere and use this to make agreed minimum repayments to your past creditors (although potentially you are robbing Peter to pay Paul).
- You can pay your creditors near enough on time, but only by increasing your overdraft facility or taking new loans.

 Proceed with extreme caution

- You are not able to pay creditors within agreed terms and they have put you on stop; but they have agreed to give you longer to make proposals to pay.
- You can only get limited credit from new sources and you are using this to fend off your existing creditors.
- If you are in business, you cannot accept new orders because you cannot get raw materials or pay for the overtime to complete them.
- Your bank has decided to claw back your overdraft facility and you are having to miss payments to non-essential creditors.
- Creditors are threatening legal action.

Stop NOW and seek professional advice

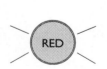

- You are on stop and can't get more credit from anywhere.
- You are regularly receiving county court **claims**, **default notices** and **statutory demands**.
- If you are in business, you are on stop with key suppliers, cannot raise working capital to fund your

order book and turnover has dropped to below break-even point.

o   With interests and penalties, your income is never going to be sufficient to meet your outgoings.

o   You are afraid to open your mail or answer the telephone.

o   You are having sleepless nights and are on medication to steady your nerves.

The trouble with borrowing

'Incur credit' may sound more business-like than 'go into debt', but it amounts to the same thing. You are supplied with money, goods or services for which you promise to pay later. When 'later' arrives and you are unable to keep your promise, make no bones about it – *you are in debt.*

Card tricks

If you played your cards right (a pretty play on words), you could run up several big credit card, store card and catalogue debts, transfer the balances to some of the many credit card companies panting for your custom, and get a six-month breathing space at a very low interest rate before the normal punitive APR kicks in, by which time you will have transferred to yet another lender. Great stuff, you may think – until something happens that brings your house of cards crashing down (see also 'Credit-surfing', p 54).

The authors regularly see individuals with considerable debts on their credit cards. The 'record' so far is approximately £120,000 for an individual with an average income. Frank Brumby has also advised an individual who was earning £800 per month and had £86,000 on credit cards. Whilst he had had a few nice holidays, he had very little to show for it!

Or to use another metaphor – some people's financial affairs are a meringue: smooth and attractive on the outside, but hollow. One swift blow and you're through the thin crust to the yawning space beneath. Is this you?

Carry on borrowing?

Deciding whether you should:

o   continue to borrow, and work your way out of financial difficulty (which if you can do it is in everybody's interests); or

o   stop borrowing and face up to your financial circumstances,

is particularly difficult, as your decision will inevitably be judged by others who have the benefit of hindsight. As we said before, the spectator gets the best view.

No two sets of circumstances are exactly the same. But at the end of the day you have to let your head rule your heart and make a realistic appraisal of whether you are going to be able to repay the money that you are about to borrow. If the answer is that:

o   you think there is a reasonable chance that you will be able to pay; *and*

o   your friends and advisers agree there is a reasonable chance,

then it is probably OK to borrow the money. However, if the answer is that you can't see how you will be able to pay back your loan on the terms it is being offered barring a lottery win or some other windfall, then you probably should not borrow more money – certainly not without explaining your circumstances to your intended creditor.

So here you are on this monstrous merry-go-round, and you want to get off. If you are in business, the decision to stop incurring additional credit can be near impossible – and in practice this decision is (wrongly) often simply avoided altogether until a creditor gets impatient and forces the pace.

People in business have a particularly hard time. Customers, suppliers and employees are all relying on your business continuing to trade, that big order or business sale could be just round the corner, and you owe it to everyone including yourself to pull off whatever is necessary.

It is a difficult decision. After all, you wouldn't have gone into business in the first place if you weren't something of an optimist.

Pause for another quote about Mr Micawber, the eternal optimist:

'I have known him come home to supper with a flood of tears, and a declaration that nothing was now left but a jail; and go to bed making a calculation of the expense of putting bow-windows to the house "in case anything turned up".'

Today, for 'bow-windows' read 'UPVC windows' or 'a conservatory'. Does it sound familiar?

But, however sure you are that something will turn up, there comes a point when you drive through the amber light (see above), where you know (or ought to know, if you can bring yourself to think about it at all) that there is no reasonable prospect that you, or your business, can avoid going into some form of insolvency. At this point (which may be different from the point where you and your business are actually insolvent – see below) you should slam on the brakes:

o   stop borrowing; *and*

o   seek specialist advice from a reputable debt advice service (see 'Useful contacts'), a lawyer or a **Licensed Insolvency Practitioner**.

Until you do both of these things, the only really safe option is to go into a holding pattern where you explore the available options.

Of course, many insolvent individuals and businesses do get their finances back in order and avoid formal insolvency altogether; but for every one that does, two probably fail to do so.

In the maze of insolvency, the biggest problem is stopping, looking round and accepting that you have taken a wrong turning in the first place.

Survival strategies for small businesses

Without getting too technical, **insolvency** for businesses, like insolvency for individuals, is defined by two tests:

o   inability to pay debts as and when they fall due (known as the cash flow test); and/or

o   the moment at which **liabilities** exceed the value of **assets** (known as the balance sheet test).

The cash flow test

The court will require evidence that you are insolvent on this basis. A creditor need only establish that:

o   you owe a creditor £750 or more; and

o   the creditor issued a **statutory demand** which was not satisfied.

A statutory demand is a formal demand for a debt to be paid within 21 days. If you do not pay the debt, then the court will accept that you cannot pay your debts as and when they fall due. It is no coincidence that these are also the prerequisites for bankruptcy.

The balance sheet test

When dealing with a business, this test is more problematical. If you are in business, then your balance sheet should be prepared on a 'going concern' basis with assets shown in accordance with normal accounting conventions at cost or net realisable value, whichever is lower.

However, by definition if a business goes into a formal insolvency procedure it is *not* a going concern and at this stage the balance sheet has to be prepared on a 'break up' basis. So you value all your assets at what they might fetch at auction; and alongside you list your liabilities, including contingent liabilities like damages claims under contracts, redundancy costs and future liabilities under finance and lease agreements.

The difference between these two bases – 'going concern' and 'break up' – is like the difference between a car purring along the road, all taxed and insured, and a rotting pile of junk in a field. But if you are in doubt whether your business is a going concern, you are pretty much obliged to assume that a break up basis is appropriate and unless your balance sheet looks like BP's or Microsoft's, restating it on a break up basis is almost bound to show insolvency.

It's like going into a shark tank with a cut finger. The sharks smell the blood and move in for the kill. Once an individual or a business is insolvent, a turnaround or cure can be difficult to achieve, with credit that was abundantly available drying up and the available options narrowing fast. So early action to keep cash – the life blood of any business, large or small – rolling in to maintain the business as a going concern and avoid insolvency altogether is much the preferred course.

Are you a survivor?

If you are in business, you already know that any business can have a financial crisis. No business is immune from recessions, bad debts or market changes. But survivors know where they are and know where they are going. They have a clear idea of the problems they face and they have plans to deal with them. The earlier the problem is spotted the more options are available.

If you are in business and can answer 'yes' to the following questions the chances are you are a survivor:

o Do you have a current business plan including profit and loss, cash flow and balance sheet forecasts at monthly rests?

o Do you know your market and do you know why your customers buy from you and not your competitors?

o Do you have meaningful and timely management information, including management accounts?

o Is actual performance regularly reviewed against the plan?

o Does your management team meet regularly to formally review progress – or, if you are on your own, do you allocate time just to understand your financial position?

The key is to have a plan and stick to it. When money is tight the maxim is 'cash flow is king'. If you are not sure how to manage to maximise cash flow, speak to your accountant or to another successful business person who may have been through the same problems in the past. Every situation is different but here are some ideas:

o Collect money in from your customers more quickly. Basic credit control can do this. The tactics in *Debt Recovery* in the *Pocket Lawyer* series have proved their worth time and time again. But nagging for payment is not the only option – you can also change your terms of trade:

    – increase your prices but offer a discount for early settlement;

    – charge interest on late payment;

    – introduce more rigorous credit control measures like setting credit limits for each customer and sticking rigidly to them,

    and ultimately change your customers from bad payers to good payers.

o Pay your sales staff commission when your customer pays you. Over a short time this can completely change your customer profile and your bad debt record.

o Cut down on raw materials, work in progress and finished goods. This might require a complete re-think on manufacturing processes to reduce batch sizes.

- ○ Sell surplus assets, including:
  - – any scrap;
  - – machines that you no longer use; and
  - – surplus property.
- ○ Negotiate extended credit from major suppliers in return for additional business.

More business survival strategies – gurus and angels

Speak to your accountant or solicitor. They are the obvious gurus, and if they don't know the answer then they are sure to know someone who does.

If the business is under-capitalised and you need to beef up management skills, consider bringing in a Business Angel – you will have to give up part of your shareholding but it is better to have 50% of a successful business than 100% of a business that has failed. If you don't know which way to turn, contact your local Chamber of Commerce or Business Link; and if the situation is really bad, make contact with a business rescue and insolvency specialist. You should find some listed under 'Insolvency Practitioners' in your *Yellow Pages*.

7

You can't win them all, but ...

Honest failure

As we said earlier, Charles Dickens's father was imprisoned for debt. Whole families were confined in London's notorious debtors' prisons; babies were born there and old people died there. We have often thought the concept of debtors' prisons illogical, given that confining someone makes it even harder for debtors to earn a living; but the theory was that their friends and relations would club together to pay the debts and spring their dear ones from jail.

The bad old days are long gone. Since the latter part of the 1990s the emphasis has been on rescue rather than reprisals, and on giving debtors a fresh start.

More recently, changes made to **insolvency** law by the bringing into force of the Enterprise Act 2002 make the government's philosophy very clear. The changes reject the proposition that a **debtor**, by becoming insolvent, ceases to be someone in whom society can have trust and confidence. Instead, they recognise that honest failure is an inevitable part of a dynamic market economy. You can't fail unless you try, and it is wrong to penalise someone for trying and failing.

The overall direction of government thinking is to encourage enterprise and move towards the USA model that encourages risk-taking and sees experience of managing business failures as a core business competency. But balanced against this is a toughened regime of restrictions on bankrupts whose conduct has been irresponsible, reckless or otherwise culpable (see p 127 for a summary of the new bankruptcy offences and **bankruptcy restriction orders**).

You owe it to your creditors!

If you get into financial difficulty it is your duty to act in the best interests of your **creditors**. You have had the use of their money and they will suffer if you go bust. Most of what you should and shouldn't be doing is common sense. Here are some pointers.

Do's and don't's

Do:

o   Take stock of your situation.

o   Talk to your advisor or a valued friend.

o   Understand how you got into your current situation.

o   Prepare a plan for at least the next few months.

o   Be realistic.

o   Ask your accountant or lawyer to recommend a **Licensed Insolvency Practitioner**.

Don't:

o   Incur more credit needlessly.

o   Lie awake and worry – share the problem with an advisor or a valued friend.

o   Treat one creditor more favourably than another or attempt to hide assets from your creditors.

o   Ignore threats of legal action from creditors.

Acting in your creditors' interests would usually involve:

o   not incurring further credit (OK, not borrowing any more money!); and

o   taking steps to increase your income and reduce your outgoings,

so that you can repay the debt you have incurred.

Beware of dodgy debt advice

The Insolvency Helpline website speaks for all responsible advisers when it warns against what they call cowboy debt advice (see www.insolvencyhelpline.co.uk/beware/beware-bad-advice.htm).

They say: 'The real truth about debt and credit problems is that you can achieve financial freedom through a professionally managed plan; however, you can also make your financial situation much worse by signing up with the wrong company. Just use common sense; if it sounds too good to be true, it probably is.'

You need to know the difference between professionals and volunteers who have your interests at heart, and people whose 'help' will cost you money and may well make your problems worse. Debt management companies spend thousands of pounds a week on advertising. Ask yourself how they get the money to pay for this.

Talk to the Licensed Insolvency Practitioner

Nothing in the world will keep you and your business afloat if your **debts** are dragging you down. You need rescuing – fast. So you call in a **Licensed Insolvency Practitioner (LIP)**. There are about 2,000 LIPs in the UK and approximately half of these take formal insolvency appointments. Most have wide experience of personal and corporate insolvency, and employ a mix of accounting, legal and commercial skills in a wide range of situations.

An LIP will review your financial position and set out the available options. These may involve formal insolvency procedures and, if necessary, they can guide you into one of these and then take a formal insolvency appointment. Acting in such a formal capacity, the LIP's job is to achieve a maximum realisation of your assets and then ensure an equitable distribution to your **creditors** in accordance with the law. Unlike unlicensed debt counsellors, insolvency practitioners are heavily regulated and you should feel confident that your affairs will be professionally handled.

Face facts

If you are in financial difficulty, then it is almost certain that 'no change' is not an option. You need to act to:

o   understand how you have got into the position that you are in; and

o   plan your way out of it.

In this kind of situation, no news is usually bad news – you need to monitor your progress and be realistic about what is achievable. It may be that you simply cannot plan your way out of the financial difficulties you are in without outside help and, in extreme circumstances, without a fresh start through some type of insolvency procedure.

Take control

You are probably worried, even scared. You may think you are on a collision course with oblivion – but actually it isn't that bad. As we said, get all the sound advice you can. Turn to your accountant, check out the debt advice on the web (see 'Useful contacts' for details and make sure you avoid the cowboys – see above!), turn to valued friends, especially anyone who has had similar experiences.

Borrowing more money could be the answer, but probably isn't. It is far more likely that old-fashioned adages like 'Take care of the pence and the pounds will take care of themselves', 'Cut your coat according to your cloth' and even 'A penny hained is a penny gained' will bring a reversal in your fortunes.

But always:

o   take control;

o   be proactive;

o   take advice; and then

o   be positive about what you do next.

Read on.

8

Insolvency looms – what are the options?

The 'ladder'

1   an **informal arrangement**;
2   an **administration order**;
3   an **individual voluntary arrangement** (IVA);
4   **bankruptcy**.

Think of a ladder leading down from a jetty. The bottom rung is actually under the water.

So you think you may be heading for **insolvency**. The best approach, if possible, is to deal with your debts first before spending further. If you take action early on, then you will be able to start higher up the ladder of options 1 to 4. If the debt becomes too much, you might find that you start half way down the ladder or are only left with option number 4, which is bankruptcy.

Re-financing

Could re-financing keep you afloat? You have probably seen TV commercials from debt management companies urging you to re-finance your debts. If you have several debts – credit card, catalogue, hire purchase and so on – then the most straightforward option may be to take out a loan, usually secured on your home, to clear the debts in full, leaving you with one monthly instalment to pay for the term of the loan with a lower interest charge, typically down from the high teens to below 10%. We need hardly point out that this does not actually get you out of debt!

Re-financing is not the only option; it will probably cost you more in the long run, and some people may have bad **credit ratings** (see below) and cannot easily obtain further finance.

Re-financing includes re-mortgaging. You might be tempted to re-mortgage your home if there is a decent amount of equity there.

Equity? Suppose your home is worth £120,000 on the open market and your mortgage is only £60,000. Then in theory you own £60,000 worth of equity. You might decide, on the strength of that, to take out a bigger mortgage at an interest rate which compares very favourably with your other lenders, and use the money to pay them off.

This option can work in your favour while the housing market is buoyant. On the other hand, if the housing market collapses and you are left owing more to your mortgage lender than your home is worth, you face 'negative equity' and the likelihood of losing your home if you cannot maintain the monthly mortgage payments. Moreover, remember what this represents. Suppose you bought some furniture on credit which you cannot now pay off. So you re-mortgage over 20–25 years to pay the debt. Do you really want to be paying off the furniture in 20 years' time when it might be long gone?

Credit-surfing

(See also 'Card tricks', p 41.) Some people 'credit-surf', changing their credit card after introductory offers (often at low interest rates and typically for six months) expire. There is nothing wrong with this approach; indeed many debt management companies have set up in business advising individuals to do this (and also charge a monthly fee for the privilege – see p 57). However, many people are tempted to spend money once again on the credit cards that they have not cancelled that are now free of debt.

If you transfer a balance from (say) Passport to Swordfish to take advantage of their six-month low-interest terms, cut up your Passport card so you can't be tempted to run up more debts on it. Otherwise you can find yourself caught in a terrifying spiral of ever-increasing debt.

There is another drawback to credit-surfing. If you are unable to pay the loan back within the honeymoon period, you may have to pay interest – back-dated to when you took out the agreement – so always read the small print very carefully! See p 2 for an example of Terms and Conditions which give the lie to a supposedly attractive credit card deal.

Apart from making sure you clear the debt within the six-month honeymoon period, you *must* keep good records of all payments, so that you can prove you made the payments at the allotted times. If the lender claims that you missed a payment and you can't prove them wrong, it could either cost you a lot of money or start a stressful dispute.

The next step

This depends upon the following.

o   how much you owe;

o   who your **creditors** are and how much you owe them; and

o   how much your **assets** are worth.

And you will remember that the options are, in descending order of desirability:

1   the **informal arrangement** at the top of the ladder;

2   an **administration order** on the next rung;

3   the **individual voluntary arrangement** (IVA); and

4   **bankruptcy** at the bottom of the ladder.

Informal arrangement

Advantages

○ inexpensive;

○ re-schedules payment of debts;

○ no court involvement;

○ avoids formal insolvency procedure;

○ no real stigma; and

○ credit reference agencies are not normally notified.

Disadvantages

○ requires approval by all **creditors**;

○ only appropriate if you have a limited and therefore fairly manageable number of creditors; and

○ not legally binding on creditors.

With this option, there is no need to involve the court, nor is it necessary to call in an **Insolvency Practitioner**. However, in order to make it workable, all of your creditors *must* agree to the informal arrangement. The more creditors you have, therefore, the less likely it is that you will achieve 100% support. If one single creditor does not agree, then that creditor may continue to pursue you for the debt until they are paid in full.

The problem with this, of course, is that the one creditor who refuses to accept the informal arrangement can often be the creditor who will make you bankrupt; and there is no point whatsoever in agreeing to pay off the majority of your creditors, only to find that a few months later you have been made bankrupt in any event. In those circumstances you will need to consider the other options.

You can do it!

If there are only a few creditors and the debts due to them are relatively small, then it may be possible to reach an arrangement with those creditors by agreeing to pay each creditor a lump sum from a third party, or payments over a period of time. In order to do this, you need to write to each of your creditors and explain your financial circumstances and offer terms for repayment.

We repeat: you will probably have seen advertisements on television from debt agencies who say that they can reduce your monthly payments on debts dramatically. This is no miracle cure. It is simply an **informal arrangement** where the debt agency takes stock of your income and liabilities, calculates what you can afford to pay and then writes to your creditors offering terms. The limitations and disadvantages we have just referred to are therefore the same as if you DIY.

The agency will also charge for their services, normally a percentage of your monthly payment. This is likely to mean the offer to creditors is far less (you only have a limited pot of money available), so the monthly payments either:

o   stretch out apparently forever; or

o   are higher than you can realistically afford,

which just worsens your position.

The agency will not do anything for you that you cannot do yourself.

We should also point out that many **creditors**, specifically the high street banks and Inland Revenue, dislike dealing with the debt agencies and will often refuse any deal such agencies offer on principle.

Why not do your sums, then approach all your creditors and offer a deal? We show you how to do this below.

The common approach is to prepare a statement of your income and expenditure (you can find this on p 143) on, say, a monthly basis to calculate the level of income you can afford to pay, in total, to your creditors.

You should also:

o   calculate your total debt; and

o   work out how much each creditor should be offered according to their share of the total debt.

Example

Suppose you can afford £250 per month to pay to your creditors.

You have four creditors who are due the sums of £8,000, £4,000, £3,000 and £1,000 respectively. Your total debt is therefore £16,000.

Creditor A	£8,000
Creditor B	£4,000
Creditor C	£3,000
Creditor D	£1,000
	————
Total owed	£16,000

You owe Creditor A £8,000 - half of your entire debt. So you offer Creditor A half the income (£250) you have put aside to pay debts, ie, £125 per month.

Creditor B is owed a quarter of the entire debt; you offer them £62.50

Creditor C, who is owed three-sixteenths of the entire debt, gets £46.97.

Creditor D (due £1,000) is owed one-sixteenth of your entire debt; you offer £15.63 per month.

Creditor A	£125.00 per month
Creditor B	£62.50 per month
Creditor C	£46.87 per month
Creditor D	£15.63 per month
	————
Total repayments	£250.00 per month

You should then write to your creditors offering your terms for repayment. There are various terms that can be offered, including:

o   £X per month for Y months as payment in full;

o   £X per month until debts are paid in full; or

o   a one-off lump sum.

If one or more of your creditors rejects your offer, you can always make an increased offer if your circumstances allow.

There is no point whatsoever in reaching an agreement with all your creditors, only to discover after a couple of months that you cannot afford to keep up the payments that you have promised. Another **default** will not help. Always consider very carefully how much you can afford to offer and set yourself a limit.

Secured creditors

It is particularly important to win secured creditors – the ones who hold security on their loan (such as your home) – over to your way of thinking. Let's suppose you are having problems keeping up with your mortgage repayments. A letter like the sample on p 140, supported by your income and expenditure schedule, could be effective here.

Mortgage lenders are often sympathetic if you go to them and tell them frankly that you are having difficulties with paying your mortgage. They will try to come to an arrangement with you to help you through your difficulties. However, you should always bear in mind the fact that as a mortgage lender they hold security over your home and unless they are paid in full they always have the option of repossession. All the ads for mortgages carry a warning along the lines of 'Your home may be in danger unless you keep up the payments'. They mean what they say!

Where an informal arrangement is concerned, the creditors will usually expect to be paid in full. You should also remember that the Inland Revenue and HM Customs & Excise (the VAT man) are not noted for their patience. The only terms they are likely to agree to will require payment in full, over a limited period of time. Our experience is that they will want their money within six months.

Administration orders

An informal arrangement, as its name implies, does not involve going to court. The other three options do. The first of these is an **administration order**.

Advantages

o   binding on all **creditors** even if they disagree;
o   inexpensive;
o   just one payment to the court each month;
o   avoids formal insolvency procedures; and
o   you avoid the stigma and inconvenience of bankruptcy.

Disadvantages

o   your total debts cannot be more than £5,000; and
o   you must have a **county court judgment (CCJ)** entered against you before you apply for one.

An administration order is very similar to an **informal arrangement** (see above), but it is administered by the court rather than by you. Put simply, you make payments to the court, under whatever order the judge makes, and the court distributes the money to your creditors for you. The beauty of this scheme is that all you have to worry about is making the one payment to the court.

An administration order is extremely useful where you have put an offer to your creditors under an **informal**

arrangement (see above), but you have been unable to persuade all of them to accept. This is because if the court makes an administration order, it is binding on *all* creditors – they have to play ball, like it or not.

Are you eligible for one?

The bad news is that not all debtors can apply for an administration order. This procedure is only available if:

o you have total debts of less than £5,000 (see above). The £5,000 applies to *all* debts, including any outstanding mortgage that you may have;

o you also have at least two outstanding debts, one of which must be a **county court judgment** that has been made against you.

The CCJ can often be the most difficult hurdle to overcome. It often happens that creditors prefer not to sue as this, of course, will cost them money in court fees. Instead, they may try to recover the debt by using debt collectors; and therefore no judgment is ever entered against you. In some circumstances this would be a good thing; but in this case it disqualifies you from applying to the court for an administration order.

How do I get one?

If you are eligible to apply for an administration order, then you must make an application to the court. The procedure is as follows.

o Obtain the application form (Form N92) together with the guidance notes (Form N270). You can download these forms from the Court Service website – go to www.courtservice.gov.uk and click on 'forms'.

o Complete the form.

o Take or send the papers back to the court. There is no fee when you apply, but if an order is made, the court will deduct 10% from any payments they make.

Can you DIY? If you are sensible and well organised, yes. But it is wise to get expert advice before you submit your application to the court. Your local Citizens Advice Bureau (see 'Useful contacts') will help with form-filling.

If you are on benefits you should be eligible for legal advice under the Legal Services Commission scheme. You may also be able to have a solicitor to act for you. Check out your Yellow Pages for a firm of solicitors near you.

What happens next?

The court then fixes a hearing date and notifies all your creditors for you. You must make sure, when you are filling in the application form, that you list the names and addresses of *all* your **creditors** so that they are notified, as they are all entitled to attend the hearing (although in practice few do).

You will of course need to go to the hearing, which takes place on a fairly informal basis. The case will normally be heard in the judge's chambers, which means a book-lined room with a desk for the judge and a table where you and any creditors (and their legal advisers if any) will sit.

The District Judge, when considering your application, will look at your **assets**, liabilities, income and expenditure and will then fix a monthly sum which, subject to any reviews which may take place, will be all you need to pay.

In doing all this, the District Judge will take all your financial circumstances into account. If you are genuinely hard up, the judge will set the monthly payment accordingly. It may well be a lot less than the creditors would wish for; but they are stuck with it!

You pay the money directly to the court, and the court takes its cut and then distributes the money among the creditors. The bad news is that if you get behind with your payments, your case can be referred back to the District Judge and he may well **discharge** (cancel) the administration order, leaving you at the mercy of your creditors.

Good news!

But there is good news too. Some District Judges may even put a time limit on your payments, so that in practice you do not have to pay the total amounts due to your creditors.

Another piece of good news is 'time off for good behaviour'. Suppose the court reviews the administration order and sees that you have been able to keep up your payments without defaulting. In some cases, a District Judge may **discharge** the order and declare that it has been satisfied. This means that you need make no further payments to creditors. You cannot guarantee that this will happen, but it is more common than you might think.

Individual voluntary arrangement

Whereas the court makes an **administration order** whether the **creditors** like it or not, an **individual voluntary arrangement (IVA)** involves the creditors very closely indeed. It has advantages and disadvantages.

Advantages

o   Avoids bankruptcy (and the associated stigma);
o   binding on all **creditors** even if some of them do not agree;
o   if you are a professional, will not necessarily bar you from remaining in practice;
o   your **assets** remain in your control; and
o   unanimity is not required – an IVA requires 75% in value (see below) of creditors who bother to vote to approve.

Note that the magic figure is 75% *in value* of the money you owe to those creditors who vote. The money you owe to creditors who do not vote at all is *not* included when calculating the percentages. Suppose you owe £100,000 in total and you owe £65,000 to your biggest creditor. That creditor agrees to your proposals but none of the other creditors bothers to vote. If something like that happens, you may soon be home and dry.

Disadvantages

o   Set-up costs;

o   if the IVA is not approved you are more likely to be forced into **bankruptcy** than before;

o   some creditors require a dividend of at least 25 pence in the pound regardless of your personal circumstances; and

o   it requires 75% in value of your debt (see above) to approve an IVA.

How an IVA works

Suppose your financial circumstances rule out an **administration order** (for example, you have an outstanding mortgage that takes you over the £5,000 limit – see above), and/or you are unable to reach an **informal arrangement** with your creditors. Then, in order to avoid bankruptcy, your remaining option is to propose an IVA to your **unsecured creditors** (these, you will recall, are the ones who don't hold security, such as bricks and mortar). The IVA is put forward to the creditors in a legal document which is referred to as the **Proposal**.

An IVA is a contract with all of your unsecured creditors on the one hand, and you on the other. You make a Proposal (with a capital P) about the form that contract should take. The Proposal can contain almost any terms that you would like to offer to the creditors, who can then accept it, reject it, or make counter proposals (called 'modifications'). There are also certain details that must be disclosed in the Proposal that are required by law.

Broadly speaking, the Proposal will contain terms offering either delayed or reduced payments of the debts or a lump sum in full and final settlement. For creditors to vote in favour of the Proposal, it needs to offer them a significantly better outcome than they could expect from your bankruptcy. Also, like all contracts, it needs to work for both sides: it must offer you a better deal too, such as letting you keep your home, with family and friends paying for your interest in it. Such an arrangement requires the approval of the court under the control of a **Licensed Insolvency Practitioner** (LIP), who will be called a **nominee** before a creditors' meeting and a **Supervisor** after the creditors' meeting if the IVA is approved.

Am I a good candidate for an IVA?

Not all individuals should consider an IVA. It is not appropriate for nominal or small payments to be made. It is best used where an individual:

o   can arrange for a lump sum payment (of several thousand pounds or more); *or*

o   can afford monthly payments of at least £100 per month, but usually more.

A combination of the two is ideal.

You should bear in mind that as a LIP is involved, they will need to be paid a fee. The size of the fee will depend upon how complex your circumstances are. If you are an employee and making monthly payments for the duration of the IVA, then the fee will be towards the lower end. If you are a sole trader with a complicated business, the fee may well be higher.

You should anticipate that the LIP will expect to be paid between £750 and £3,000 depending upon the complexity of your financial affairs. This may seem a lot, but bear in mind that it is the creditors who bear the cost and who benefit from a successfully implemented IVA. For this fee, the LIP will undertake all the steps up to and including the holding of the creditors' meeting (see below).

What do I do next?

If you believe that you are a good candidate for an IVA, then you should make an appointment to see a local LIP or specialist insolvency solicitor. The great majority will not charge a fee for the initial meeting. To enable the LIP to assess your position at this stage, it is very important to prepare some information for him beforehand. Ideally, try to prepare the following:

- A list of all of your **creditors**, including:
  - name;
  - address;
  - account or reference number;
  - amount owed; and
  - date the last payment was made to each creditor.

  If it is not clear from the name of the creditor what the debt is in relation to, then a brief narrative is helpful, such as 'finance outstanding on car', or 'bar tab' or 'mortgage lender'.

- A list of all your **assets**, including:
  - your home and any other properties;
  - car(s);
  - endowment policies;
  - pension policies, and so on.

  Include a brief description and try to estimate the value. If a valuation has been done, or you have a statement, that will do, even if it is 12 months old.

- A breakdown of your income and monthly expenditure (use the one provided in this book). If you are self-employed, take along the last three years' accounts if you can.

What happens next?

Assuming the LIP recommends that an IVA is appropriate, the first step will be the drafting of a written Proposal that sets out your offer and also explains why such an arrangement is desirable and why the creditors should be expected to agree to it.

Can you DIY?

No. The law when it was first enacted envisaged that you would draft the **Proposal** yourself, then approach a

LIP, who would then agree to act and report to the court on your Proposal. However, Proposals are not a DIY job, and it is common practice for the LIP or a solicitor to draft the Proposal on your behalf. The Proposal must contain, at the very least, the following details (to the best of your immediate knowledge). This list may seem quite complicated, but your LIP will work through it with you.

o   Your **assets** (see above), with an estimate of what each asset is worth.

o   The extent to which the assets are charged/secured in favour of creditors (eg, mortgages, hire-purchase, etc).

o   The extent to which particular assets are to be excluded from the IVA and why they will be excluded.

o   Details of any assets owned by other people that it is proposed to include in the IVA, the source of such assets and the terms on which they are to be made available. (A typical example of this would be if someone else offered their own assets – the catchphrase is 'third party funds'. Your parents or partner, in order to make the IVA more attractive to creditors, might offer to pay a lump sum into the IVA for the benefit of creditors, provided the creditors approved the IVA.)

o   The nature and amount of your debts and how you propose to deal with them.

o   Any guarantees that any other person may have been given in respect of your liabilities.

o   How long you propose the voluntary arrangement should go on for.

o   How much you propose to pay to the **nominee** and **Supervisor** by way of fees and expenses.

o   Whether any guarantees are to be offered by any other person and (if so) what security is to be given or sought.

o   (if applicable) The manner in which you propose to carry on your business during the term of the IVA.

o   Details of any further credit facilities required.

o   The functions of the Supervisor.

o   The name of the person proposed as Supervisor of the IVA.

Always remember that for creditors to accept an IVA, your offer must be an attractive one. You cannot, of course, exclude from an IVA assets which would become available to creditors if you were made bankrupt (unless those assets are replaced by something else of value), and then expect creditors to accept your Proposal. Why should they, if they can get a better deal by bankrupting you?

In addition to the information that the law requires you to disclose, the Proposal should also include a brief explanation of the background to your predicament and your plans for the future. This would also include provision (if this applies to you) for you to continue to trade under the IVA, as IVAs are particularly helpful to self-employed or professional people who may lose their livelihood if they were bankrupt. Indeed, some people, such as solicitors, cannot practise at all if they are **bankrupt**.

For example, a self-employed builder who was made bankrupt would find it extremely difficult to carry on trading under the restrictions imposed by bankruptcy, the main one being (as you will see below) that you may not borrow money (the law-speak is 'pledge credit') in excess of £250 without first disclosing that you are bankrupt. Of course, as soon as you tell suppliers that you are bankrupt, it is unlikely that any credit will be on offer! Paying for building materials up-front would be difficult if not impossible, thus making carrying on trading also impossible. Of course, this is not particularly satisfactory for the builder, and it is no use whatsoever to his creditors: if the builder is unable to earn, they don't get paid.

Under an IVA, however, there are no such restrictions – although you would of course continue to trade under the watchful eye of the Supervisor and subject to the terms of the Proposal. The Proposal will set out a number of provisions to allow the individual to continue to work; but it may also incorporate a number of protective measures for both the individual and the creditors to make sure that further debts are not incurred.

Safe as houses?

You may be a homeowner, and one of the main priorities will be to keep your home if possible. If there is any valuable equity in the property (in other words, if its market value is significantly greater than the amount you owe on it), then your home becomes a bargaining counter. To persuade the **creditors** to accept the **Proposal**, it must make provision, one way or another, to ensure that the value of any interest in your home is made available to creditors in some way. As your home is an **asset** that would be available to creditors if you were made bankrupt, your creditors would eventually be paid from the sale of your home – and therefore they will expect the same to happen in an IVA.

How the Proposal deals with your home depends entirely upon the value of it to creditors and the extent to which any third party, or indeed you, can account to creditors for it.

There are several options:

o   A co-owner of the property (typically your husband, wife or partner) may be able to buy you out by raising money that is then offered to the creditors in the IVA.

o   You may be able to raise finance against the value of the equity in your home, and throw that into the IVA pot.

o   In a worst-case scenario, you might have no choice but to sell the property and find somewhere else to live for yourself and your family. This can, however, be made a little easier by making it a term of the Proposal that you undertake to sell your home within one, two or three years of the IVA, in order to give you at least some time to sell the property and find suitable alternative accommodation.

o   If you are in a position where you are offering creditors payment in full, then you may be able to exclude the family home altogether.

o   By making significant contributions from earnings that you would not have been able to make if you were made bankrupt.

In summary, the Proposal should be:

o   realistic;

o   informative; *and*

o   achievable.

Remember, the earlier you seek advice, the more time you have to prepare an attractive Proposal.

Be truthful! If you make any false representations in the Proposal, you may be committing a criminal offence.

How long?

This is a difficult one. As the law stood prior to the Enterprise Act 2002, discharge from **bankruptcy** was usually after three years; two if the total debt was fairly modest. When **IVAs** were first put forward, the term of the IVA was usually three years, to mirror the bankruptcy regime which was then in force. **Creditors** have, over time, realised that a **debtor** wishing to avoid bankruptcy by putting forward an IVA may be prepared to make sacrifices.

It is current standard practice, therefore, for the term of the IVA based on contributions from future earnings to be five years, which means the debtor will possibly be paying a contribution from their income for that entire period, whereas in bankruptcy the 'sentence' might be three years at the most. For most debtors seeking an IVA, however, this is an acceptable price to pay for keeping afloat.

With the changes brought in by the Enterprise Act 2002, and **discharge** from bankruptcy for most bankrupts taking place within 12 months, this may lead to shorter IVAs, generally lasting three years rather than five years. Only time will tell. Realistically, is it worth struggling under an IVA for five years if bankruptcy lasts less than one year? Only you will know which is the more attractive option.

Once the **Proposal** has been drafted and both you and the **LIP** are happy with it, you must sign it.

At the same time as signing the Proposal, you will also sign a notice confirming your choice of **LIP** as **nominee**. The nominee will endorse this notice, at which point he will help you to **file** an application at the court.

Documents are *filed with* or *at* the court, never sent or submitted. Likewise, in Lawyerland you *serve* documents *on* other people instead of handing, faxing, posting, etc. If you are a company director you will know that Companies House also expect you to file documents with/at them. You get used to it.

The application

The following documents will need to be filed at the court. Don't worry, your **LIP**, now called the **'nominee'**, will organise all of this for you. The nominee will send to the court:

o   the court fee of £130 (which you will have already paid up front to your nominee);

o   the **Proposal**;

o   the notice your Nominee endorsed consenting to their appointment;

o   an application explaining to the court what is being asked for;

o   a supporting statement or **affidavit** setting out prescribed details. You will have signed this.

An **affidavit** has to be sworn. If you do this before a solicitor, it will normally cost you £5 plus £2 for each exhibit attached to the affidavit. A court official will do it for free.

When all the documents have been **filed**, an interim order (see below) can be granted if necessary.

Some breathing space: the interim order

Meanwhile, your **creditors** may be getting restless. It would be disastrous if they lost patience and decided to bankrupt you before you could arrange your **IVA**. So, with the help of your **nominee**, you ask the court to protect you from your creditors in the time leading up to the creditors' meeting by applying for what is known as an 'interim order' at the same time as **filing** the documents above.

The interim order effectively prevents all creditors, including landlords, Inland Revenue and HM Customs & Excise, from suing you or pursuing you any further for the debts during the run-up to the creditors' meeting, and allows time for the **Proposal** to be considered by your nominee and then placed before the creditors for their approval at the meeting.

Bear in mind that you can only apply for one interim order in any period of 12 months. Please also note that recent changes brought into force by the Insolvency Act 2000 (which did not come into force itself until 1 January 2003) now permit you to propose an IVA without an interim order. This may be helpful in limited circumstances which are beyond the scope of this book (seek professional advice) or where no particular creditor is applying any real pressure. The procedure is the same, except that no interim order is granted by the court.

Nominee's report

○ After lodging the application, the **nominee** must then prepare and **file** a report with the court within 14 days, although this can be extended if necessary. The nominee must report to the court as to whether he believes the **Proposal** is worth being considered by your **creditors**. In doing so, he must remain independent and consider whether the proposals are fair, feasible, provide creditors with proper information to be able to consider them and, most importantly, if implemented have a realistic prospect of being achieved. Please note that sometimes the nominee's report can be filed at the same time as the application and is known by insolvency practitioners colloquially as a 'concertina order'. Nobody seems to know why!

o   Assuming that the court is satisfied with the nominee's report, the interim order will then be extended (if one has been applied for), until after the creditors' meeting.

o   The nominee will then send a notice, enclosing the Proposal, to all known creditors, at least 14 days before the creditors' meeting is to be held. The notice is accompanied by forms (called a 'proof of debt' form and a 'proxy' form) which will enable a creditor to vote either by post or in person, or indeed to appoint someone (a proxy) to vote on their behalf.

Important: you must give details of *all* creditors. A creditor who does not receive notice of the meeting is a loose cannon. That creditor can take you to court if they feel hard done by.

The creditors' meeting

The meeting itself must be held at a convenient venue for **creditors** between 10 am and 4 pm on any business day. It will be chaired by the **nominee** or one of his staff, who will be called the Chairman. You will need to attend.

It is quite normal for no creditors to turn up at the meeting, especially if all of your creditors are major financial institutions. The meeting, therefore, may consist of only you and the nominee! However, if creditors do turn up, they have the opportunity to question you about your financial affairs. Sometimes, a creditor may get stroppy and may make their feelings known quite forcefully, which may not be to your liking. However, you should bear in mind that you are asking your creditors, by putting forward an **IVA**, to forgo and/or wait for some of the money you owe them. The least you can do, therefore, is allow them to let off some steam.

You will have realised by now that a **Licensed Insolvency Practitioner** can wear many different hats. According to the kind of insolvency problems being handled, an LIP can be a **Trustee in Bankruptcy**, a **Nominee**, a **Supervisor**, a **Receiver**, a **Liquidator**, an Office Holder – and of course a Chairman (see above). Thankfully, the LIP only charges one fee!

Creditors are entitled to vote, provided they have given the Chairman written notice of their claim either before or at the meeting. There is no requirement for proxy forms to be submitted before the meeting; the proxy holder may take the form to the meeting itself.

Votes at the meeting are then calculated according to the *amount* that is owed to a creditor. If secured creditors are satisfied that all of the debt is covered by their security, they do not vote in the IVA. If the secured creditors believe that their security is worth less than their debt, they may value their security and vote for what is called the *unsecured balance*.

For example, if you own a house worth £75,000, but it has a mortgage secured against it for £100,000, the mortgage lender may decide to vote at the IVA meeting for a sum of up to £25,000, as this is the sum the mortgage lender will be out of pocket if the house is sold for £75,000. That £25,000 is the *unsecured balance*.

For the Proposal to be approved, more than 75% of the creditors, in value, need to vote in favour of your Proposal. Therefore the nominee will only look at the votes for and against the Proposal and will ignore any creditors who have not voted at all. So if you owe a total of £120,000, and only £100,000 worth of creditors vote at all, you need in excess of £75,000 worth of votes to get your IVA approved (£75,000.01 will be enough!). The £20,000 of creditors who did not vote are not included in the calculation. They will, however, still be bound by the IVA.

Creditors who do not attend will normally appoint the Chairman of the meeting to vote on their behalf, ie, as their proxy holder. The Chairman votes as directed on the proxy form to reject or accept the proposal, with or without modifications.

Counter proposals or 'modifications'

The **Proposal** itself, as we said before, sets out a simple contract between the individual **debtor** and the **creditors**. The debtor is offering certain terms to the creditors; and therefore the creditors can make counter proposals called 'modifications'. It may, therefore, be the case that a creditor will vote in favour of a Proposal only if certain modifications to the original Proposal are agreed. At that time, depending upon whether or not sufficient votes have been received, it will be for you to decide whether or not to agree to the modifications put forward. Some of these modifications might be quite onerous.

The meeting itself may be adjourned (as many times as may be required) until the Proposal is either accepted or rejected; but no adjourned meeting may be held more than 14 days after the original meeting.

Following the acceptance or rejection of the Proposal by the creditors, the Chairman will prepare a report on the meeting and **file** a copy with the court within four days of the final meeting.

The Chairman will also set out in the report how creditors voted. If the Proposal is approved, the Chairman must lodge details of the **IVA** with the Secretary of State and the information will then be included in a register which is available for public inspection. Although it is not advertised in the press, the IVA is therefore on public record and may show up on any credit search that is undertaken. More about this register in 'Useful contacts'.

Within 28 days of the report on the creditors' meeting being filed with the court, an application can be made by any of the creditors who wishes to challenge the decision, on the grounds that:

o   the IVA approved at the meeting or any adjourned meeting is against the interests of a particular creditor or group of creditors; or

o   there has been some material irregularity at, or in relation to, the meeting.

If the court upholds the challenge, it may give directions (other people instruct or give instructions; courts always direct or give directions) that a further meeting should be held to consider a revised Proposal, or that the meeting should be reconvened to hear the original Proposal once again. The court may also order that the Proposal is not binding on a particular creditor or hold the Proposal invalid altogether.

Approved – what then?

When the **IVA** has been approved, your versatile insolvency practitioner, the erstwhile **nominee**, will take off the Chairman's hat and don **Supervisor** headgear. The Supervisor will then supervise the IVA in accordance with the terms of the **Proposal**. You must comply with your obligations under the Proposal, otherwise the Supervisor may fail it. Every 12 months they must prepare a summary of the money they have received and what they have paid out, and send a copy to the court, the **creditors**, and you. The Supervisor is also under the supervision of the court and may apply to the court for directions on any matter relating to the IVA.

Once the IVA has been completed, the Supervisor reports on this to the creditors. We say blithely 'once the IVA has been completed', but this is like saying 'Time passed and the tiny sapling grew into a mighty oak'. Read on.

To persuade creditors to accept the voluntary arrangement Proposal, you must offer creditors more than they could realistically expect to receive in the event of bankruptcy.

This can often mean:

o agreeing with the creditors that the IVA will continue for longer than a bankruptcy would – such as three/four/five years rather than as little as one year for a bankruptcy; or

o introducing money from a third party (such as from friends or family) into the arrangement, which would not be available to creditors in a bankruptcy.

It often happens, however, that despite an extended period and/or the introduction of third party funds, the creditors will not get paid in full. Under the IVA, however, in approving the arrangement, creditors are agreeing to accept whatever they receive under the terms of the Proposal in full and final settlement of the debtor's liabilities and the advantage of this, therefore, is that an individual can achieve a 'clean slate' at the end of it – provided that the arrangement has been implemented successfully.

Variation

It is almost impossible for the terms of the voluntary arrangement to cover every conceivable change of circumstances. Some events might occur which mean that the **IVA** can be finished early; others may mean that the IVA needs to be extended.

Hopefully the **Proposal**, if drafted by a responsible insolvency practitioner, will permit a further **creditors'** meeting to be called at any time to consider a 'variation' or change of the terms of the arrangement.

If you wish to consider a variation to the terms of your IVA, you should contact the **Supervisor** of the IVA immediately. You will need to explain why the variation is required. Your proposed variation will then be circulated to all of your creditors, who will be entitled to vote on it in a similar fashion to the first meeting of creditors.

Such variation will need to be approved by the usual 75% majority, and if it is not, then you will be stuck with the original terms. Bear in mind that if you have defaulted on the original terms (see below) and the variation has not been approved, you will more than likely find yourself the subject of a bankruptcy petition.

Default

There is always a risk that, for one reason or another, you cannot comply with the terms of the IVA – most commonly, you fall behind with the monthly instalments you offered to make. In such circumstances, and where the creditors are not prepared to excuse the **default**, it will be necessary for the **Supervisor** to don yet another hat and **petition** for your bankruptcy. *It is therefore vital that the terms you offer in an IVA are achievable.*

But if the terms are achievable, and you manage to keep to your side of the bargain, you will have avoided bankruptcy, which is the final option.

IVAs are a lot less common than bankruptcies. At the time of going to press, the Insolvency Service statistics online only go from 1997 to 2002. Out of 30,587 personal insolvencies in England and Wales in 2002, just 6,296 took the form of IVAs, compared with 24,291 **bankruptcy orders**.

Going bankrupt

At the bottom of the insolvency ladder we find **bankruptcy**.

Advantages

○ Brief – unless you have been up to no good;

○ once you are **discharged** you will be released from all but a few specific debts;

○ after your discharge you will, in general, have a clean slate;

○ you should not be chased by **creditors**; and

○ the **bailiffs** can't take your household contents.

Disadvantages

○ You will lose control of your **assets**;

○ the **bankruptcy restriction order**, which means:

   – until you are discharged, the amount of credit you can obtain will be restricted;

   – until you are discharged, you will be restricted on how you conduct your business in the future; and

○ even after you are discharged you will have a bad **credit rating**;

○ income payment orders and arrangements can go on for over three years, even after your discharge.

When is bankruptcy appropriate?

Bankruptcy is often the last resort and applies where no meaningful proposals can be offered to **creditors**; that is:

o   you have no valuable **assets**;

o   your income is low; or

o   not enough creditors will accept any other proposals you have put forward. In particular, a major creditor who is owed more than 25% of your debt may simply refuse your proposals for an **IVA** as a matter of principle, leaving you with no option but to go bankrupt.

Jump or be pushed?

There are two ways in which you can go **bankrupt**:

1   Jump: you present your own petition ('a debtor's **petition**') to the court. Or

2   Be pushed: a creditor, to whom you owe £750 or more, presents a petition to the court ('a creditor's petition').

Contrary to popular belief, once the bankruptcy order has been made, the effects are the same whether you jump or are pushed. There is no significant difference in attitude or leniency shown by the Official Receiver. Until recently (regardless of whether you jumped or were pushed), the amount you owed had a bearing on the length of time you remained bankrupt. That disappeared under the new legislation as from 1 April 2004. Before then, if your debts were less than £20,000 you would be discharged after two years rather than three. Now the general rule is one year.

Whether you petition for your own bankruptcy or wait for a creditor to **present** a petition against you will depend on your particular circumstances.

For example, if you are under pressure from creditors and have no alternative (see p 53) you may wish to jump; otherwise, creditors are normally only likely to consider presenting a petition for bankruptcy if they believe that you have assets that would benefit them, as bankrupting you will cost a creditor legal fees as well as court fees, time and energy (it usually costs between

£1,000 and £2,000 to make someone else bankrupt, so it is not done lightly!).

Some creditors, however, such as the Inland Revenue and certain nationwide suppliers, will present a bankruptcy petition as a matter of policy if you have a debt of £750 or more with them, whatever the circumstances. It may, however, be some time before a petition is presented.

Take advice

The implications of bankruptcy are far reaching; so before presenting your own debtor's petition, you ought to seek advice from a **Licensed Insolvency Practitioner (LIP)** or a solicitor, particularly if you have assets. In fact, the court may not make a **bankruptcy order** unless you have received advice about insolvency or, at the very least, you fully appreciate what you are letting yourself in for.

Don't let the thought of fees put you off seeking professional advice. Most **Licensed Insolvency Practitioners** will offer a free 'diagnostic' session. And the Legal Services Commission (see 'Useful contacts') enables solicitors who are part of its scheme to give free advice and assistance to clients who would normally be unable to afford legal fees. The Citizens Advice Bureau (CAB) can also assist free of charge (see 'Useful contacts').

Jumping into bankruptcy

Once you have decided that bankruptcy is for you, you can DIY and the courts are accustomed to what they call 'litigants in person'. To **file** your own **petition** you need the right forms. These are:

o   the debtor's petition; *and*

o   the Statement of Affairs.

You have two options here. You can download the documents (Form 6.27 (the petition) – see page 149 – and Form 6.28 (the Statement of Affairs) – see page 151) and the accompanying Guidance Notes (you'll need them) from the Insolvency Service website (see 'Useful contacts') or go along to your local county court, collect the paper versions and enlist the help of one of the clerks (see below).

The petition itself is quite short, but the Statement of Affairs runs to 10 pages and can be difficult to complete, although the Insolvency Service do provide a guide and some explanatory notes on how to complete the forms.

It is important to complete these documents as accurately as possible, as the court may reject an incorrectly completed application and send you home to do it properly. More importantly, you are required to give full disclosure of your affairs in the documents, otherwise you may be guilty of a criminal offence.

The good news is that:

o   there is probably someone at your local CAB who will help you to complete the forms;

o   court staff are ace at form-filling and will usually be pleased to check your paperwork for you.

Once you have completed the forms, they must then be **filed** with the court. You should attend at your local county court, basically the court that you have lived nearest to in the preceding six months. All this means is that you must send or take the papers to the court, together with the court fee in cash. (Why cash? Well, would *you* accept a cheque from someone who is about to swear to the court that they cannot pay their debts?)

At the time of going to press, the fee is £450: £140 court fee and £310 deposit for the **Official Receiver**, although you may be eligible to pay a reduced fee (£250) if you are receiving state benefits. You should check with the court whether the reduced fee applies to you, so that you know how much money you will need to pay when you file the papers. If it does, there is another form (EX160) to fill in. You can download Form EX160 from the Court Service website (www.courtservice.gov.uk and click on 'Forms'), or pick one up from the court.

As we said, one of the forms you must complete is a Statement of Affairs, which sets out your **assets** and liabilities. You will see that the Statement of Affairs includes an **affidavit**, which is a sworn statement.

The word **affidavit** is pure Latin. It comes from *affidare* – to declare (on oath) – and means 'He, she or it has declared'.

This document must be sworn – formally declared to be true – before the court will accept it. This means that, when you **file** the papers with the court, you must swear on the Bible (or the Q'ran if you are a Muslim), before an officer of the court, that the contents of the Statement of Affairs are true – hence the importance of completing the documentation accurately.

Bankruptcy while you wait?

Once you have filed the bankruptcy papers and paid the fee, the court will then tell you when you must appear before the District Judge. How long you will have to wait for a hearing depends entirely upon the court in which you have **filed** your own **petition** and how busy everyone is.

Most county courts offer a 'same-day service', especially if you attend at the court first thing in the morning (courts open for business at 10 am). You can therefore go in and file your Petition in Bankruptcy on any working day and get your **bankruptcy order** on the same day. In this instance, you will usually be asked to wait until a District Judge is available to see you later that day; and you will not necessarily be given a specific time for a hearing, so it pays to take something to read while you are waiting.

In other cases, the court clerk may set a date for a hearing, normally a few days later depending on how busy the court is, for you to return to the court for the hearing of the bankruptcy petition.

The District Judge will normally hear your bankruptcy petition in chambers (see p 63). There are no courtroom dramas. When you appear before the District Judge there should be nobody else present except the two of you.

The District Judge will read through your Petition and Statement of Affairs and may ask you one or two questions while considering whether or not to make a bankruptcy order. These questions are likely to centre on whether or not you understand the implications of what you are doing and, more importantly, whether you have received professional advice.

Normally, if you are able to confirm that you have received advice, then the chances are that the District Judge will make you bankrupt there and then, and the whole hearing will take no more than a few minutes. The District Judge will then ask you to go back to the court office and wait for your order to be typed up.

If the District Judge believes that bankruptcy is not appropriate, they may refer the matter to a **Licensed Insolvency Practitioner** for them to prepare a report to the court. This power is only exercised on very rare occasions, however, and your debts will need to be less than £40,000 and assets valued at more than £4,000. Alternatively, if the District Judge is not convinced that you have been properly advised before taking this step, you may be sent away to get some legal advice.

Being pushed into bankruptcy

Any **creditor** may **petition** for your bankruptcy – that is, apply to the court to make you bankrupt – if:

o   you owe them £750 or more; *and*

o   that sum remains unpaid.

The creditor does not necessarily have to obtain a **county court judgment (CCJ)** against you for debt before petitioning for your bankruptcy, unless the debt is the subject of a dispute between you and the creditor.

Please also note that two or more creditors can join forces to combine the debts and if the total debt comes to £750 or more they can present a joint petition.

There may be an element of spite or revenge in choosing to **bankrupt** an individual rather than sue him for **debt**. Not all insolvencies are the result of honest failure. We know of a rogue letting agent whose debts, when her case finally reached the **Official Receiver**, ran to 12 pages. Other **creditors** shrugged their shoulders. Mrs R bankrupted the agent because, as well as owing Mrs R £1,200, which Mrs R could afford to lose, the debtor had cheated Mrs R's gardener out of £50, which was a lot of money to him. That £50 proved to Mrs R that this person should be put out of business for the good of the community. She also made a point of informing the police and urging them to take action. The rogue agent was later convicted of theft.

Pay up – or else!

The quickest way is for the **creditor** to serve a **statutory demand** on you; and if you do not pay the sum demanded within 21 days the creditor is then entitled, if they wish, to present a bankruptcy **petition** against you.

For form anoraks, the statutory demand is Form 6.1 if the creditor does not already have a CCJ against you, Form 6.2 if they have one. You will find samples of the forms on pp 180 and 185.

The creditor is under a duty to do all that is reasonable to effect **personal service** of the statutory demand on you – they might do it themselves, but normally they will pay a process server to locate you and hand the demand to you personally, failing which it will be sent to you by first class post.

What can you do?

If you dispute the grounds of the **debt**, you can apply to the court to **set aside** the **statutory demand** within 18 days of the date of service. However, your dispute *must* reduce the debt to below £750, otherwise a bankruptcy **petition** may still follow and the application to set aside the statutory demand will fail.

Example: if the creditor is claiming £1,000 in the statutory demand, and you say that only £800 is due, then you can still be made bankrupt. It is only if you can prove that the debt is less than £750 that you can avoid bankruptcy. Don't forget that other creditors can always join forces and present a joint petition (see above).

This leads to an important point – *if a **statutory demand** is served on you and you pay enough to reduce the debt below £750, then a bankruptcy **petition** cannot be presented against you*. The reason for this is that it is a condition that you owe £750 or more at the date the bankruptcy petition is presented by the **creditor**.

For example, you owe £1,000 but pay £251, reducing the debt to £749. However, be careful:

o   Don't cut it too close though, just in case you have calculated the debt wrongly – reduce the debt to £700 just to be on the safe side.

o   Furthermore, if the bankruptcy petition has already been filed and you then reduce the debt below £750, the court still has the discretion to make a bankruptcy order (because you were too late in reducing the **debt**).

If you manage to 'pull a fast one' and prevent the creditor from presenting a bankruptcy petition, the creditor can still – if they already have, or later obtain, a CCJ – use other **enforcement** measures such as the **bailiff** to chase the rest of the debt. You can find more about the various enforcement measures from the creditor's point of view in *Debt Recovery* in the *Pocket Lawyer* series.

Bankruptcy petition

Assuming you do not pay the sum demanded and it is at least £750, your **creditor** can present a bankruptcy **petition** and get it **personally served** on you once again. When a creditor presents a bankruptcy petition to the court, they pay the appropriate fee (the court fee is £480 for a creditor!) and the court then seals (ie, stamps with the court logo) the petition document and returns it to the creditor for service.

The 'presentation date' is a key date. On presentation, the court will also send a notice to the Chief Land Registrar, who will cause a 'pending action' entry to be registered in the Land Charges Register. If you are trying to sell a property at the time, the purchaser's solicitors should, and nearly always will, check this Register and will see that a petition is outstanding against you. This will inevitably cause the sale to fall through or, at the very least, be held up until the bankruptcy petition is resolved.

A land charge is, of course, like a mortgage on a piece of real estate, with the creditor in the role of the mortgage lender. One of us once advised a lady in matrimonial proceedings whose husband had borrowed money to bolster his business and had a charge put on the family home as a result. The poor lady said, 'It's all right, it's only a land charge, and we don't have any land – we live in a third floor flat'!

The creditor must (law-speak again) effect **personal service** of the petition on you and a **bankruptcy order** cannot be made until such service is effected. However, if you try to avoid personal service this will not ultimately prevent the bankruptcy proceedings from continuing.

A process server will usually try to contact you by calling in person at a known address. This may include a work address if it is known, which may be embarrassing for you. If you are not there the process server may try again later, or leave a note of their contact number.

If you continue to evade the process server, the creditor may make a further application to court for 'substituted service' of the petition. In other words, the court will authorise the creditor to simply send it by first class post to a certain address or even advertise it in the local press rather than personally serve it. This will be deemed to be adequate service to enable the court to make a bankruptcy order. Please also note that if you are looking to settle the debt eventually, then evading service will simply increase the creditor's costs, which will have to be paid before withdrawing the petition.

The petition must be served at least 14 days before the day listed for the bankruptcy petition hearing (when the bankruptcy order can be made).

The petition will:

o contain the grounds upon which the creditor believes they are entitled to bankrupt you; and

o set a date for the hearing of the petition.

If you do not attend, it is extremely likely that a bankruptcy order will be made against you in your absence.

You can attend at court and make proposals to pay the creditor – proposals that the creditor may or may not accept. If you offer **security**, such as a **charge** over your home, which can be shown to be worth more than the debt due, and the creditor unreasonably rejects that offer, you may be able to get the petition thrown out.

You can find a sample creditor's bankruptcy petition on p 189.

Can I grab some breathing space?

It may be possible to ask for an adjournment of the petition hearing for three to four weeks if:

o you are likely to be in a position to pay the debt in the following few weeks; *and*

o you can provide documentary proof to the court.

In some cases the **creditor** may agree to the adjournment. Sometimes they may not, in which case you will have to try to persuade the District Judge to grant an adjournment. Frank Brumby has, on a couple of occasions, managed to get four or five adjournments in a row, although this is rare and depends upon the particular circumstances of each case.

If you have a bankruptcy petition served on you and don't believe that you should be made bankrupt, you must take legal advice and go to the court hearing, otherwise a **bankruptcy order** will be made in your absence and it may be too late. It may also cost you a great deal more than the original petition debt as an application may need to be made to annul the bankruptcy order (see p 129).

With bankruptcy, as with flu, there's a lot of it about. The table below comes from The Insolvency Service website (see 'Useful contacts'). The figures show that there is an upward trend, from 19,892 bankruptcy orders in 1997 to 24,292 in 2002 (the latest figures available).

Individual Insolvencies in England and Wales: 1997 to 2002

Type of insolvency	1997	1998	1999	2000	**2001**	**2002**
Total	24,441	24,549	28,806	29,528	**29,775**	**30,587**
Bankruptcy Orders	19,892	19,647	21,61	21,550	**23,477**	**24,292**
Individual Voluntary Arrangements	4,541	4,901	7,195	7,978	**6,298**	**6,295**

At the time of going to press the 2003 figures look disturbing. For the third quarter of 2003 alone there were 9,904 individual insolvencies (bankruptcies and **IVAs**), an increase on the second quarter of 2003 and an increase of 16.9% on the same period in 2002.

Interlude: practical matters

There are some practical matters that you should be aware of before you become subject to a **bankruptcy order**:

o   Has your partner made a will? If you own property jointly, even though there is no equity in it at present, some form of life cover is usually required by your mortgage lender so that if, for example, something happens to you or your partner, the house will be free of mortgage. Unless your partner has made a will cutting you out, your partner's share of the house comes to you and in practice is likely to go straight to the **Trustee in Bankruptcy**. You can learn more about this in *Wills and Estate Planning* in the *Pocket Lawyer* series.

o   Have your parents made a will? We mentioned this on p xxxiii but make no apology for referring to it again. Do they realise that unless they are careful they will be leaving their money to your Trustee? Money left in a will to a bankrupt is normally money down the drain. The legacy will go towards paying off the debts and the intended beneficiary will get nothing (unless, of course, the legacy is enough to pay off all the beneficiary's debts and still leave something over).

In order to avoid this situation, it is sensible to speak to anybody who you think may leave you any money and ask them to make a will to ensure that you do not receive any inheritances during the time you are bankrupt.

The classic solution is what is called a 'protective trust'. This gives the beneficiary the right to income for life, but in the event of bankruptcy the right to income is replaced by a discretionary trust. There may be other, simpler solutions – for example, leaving money to the bankrupt's partner or children.

If you have children and your family wish to leave what they have to them, there is no problem with this. If the children are under 18 they will need trustees/guardians, and as long as the will makes it clear that you are only a trustee/guardian, you can hold money or property on trust for your children. You can read about this in detail in *Wills and Estate Planning* in the *Pocket Lawyer* series.

○ In whose name are the gas, electricity, telephone and water bills at home? If any of the services is in your name, change over as soon as possible. The reason for this is that the electricity company, for example, will be told by the **Official Receiver** that you are bankrupt. They may not be happy about continuing to supply you with electricity on a quarterly account, even though you have always paid your bills. Instead, they will install a prepayment meter, which may not be convenient for you and will probably cost you more.

So, to avoid any hassle, you need to put all these services into somebody else's name, such as your partner's, before the bankruptcy order is made. The procedure is quite simple in most cases. Simply complete the relevant application form as if you were moving house; or sometimes a telephone call to the supplier is sufficient to get the account transferred. The person whose name goes on to the account may have to fill in his own form, as if they were moving into the house for the first time, and from that time onwards the bills will come addressed to that person.

At the end of the day, the supplier does not mind who pays the bill as long as it is paid.

o Beware of debts for which your partner or anyone else will be 'jointly and severally liable'.

If your partner or anyone else is jointly liable for any debts – for example, a joint bank account which is overdrawn – the creditor, though unable to pursue *you* for the debt (because you are bankrupt), is perfectly entitled to pursue your co-debtor not only for one-half of the debt, but for *all of it*.

As soon as they receive a Notice from the Official Receiver informing them that you are bankrupt, such creditors are likely to swing into action against any co-debtors; and in these circumstances you should offer terms to the relevant creditors as soon as is humanly possible. The creditor will usually be entitled to pursue the co-debtor for the full amount; and your co-debtor should seek legal advice.

'His and hers' bankruptcies

It is common for both husband and wife or pairs of partners to go bankrupt at the same time. The only difficulty with this is that banking arrangements sometimes become difficult. This is because both individuals' bank accounts will be frozen and, until new bank accounts are opened, this may cause chaos with direct debits, etc for utility bills and mortgage payments.

If you are considering joint bankruptcies, it is wise to plan ahead and consider getting professional advice. It is also worth considering the timing of the bankruptcies, possibly over a couple of months. Here's an example of this:

o Ensure all the direct debits, standing orders, wages etc are transferred to the wife's account.

○ Let the husband go bankrupt first. His bank account will be frozen; he can then open a new one and arrange for all the direct debits, etc to be transferred to his new bank account from the wife's account.

○ The wife can then go bankrupt and her account (which is no longer needed) will be frozen.

Enter the Official Receiver

Whether you jumped and bankrupted yourself, or whether you were pushed, you will be required to deal with the **Official Receiver (OR)**.

If you jumped, then arrangements will be made after the bankruptcy hearing for the OR's office to telephone you at an agreed time. You will also receive some forms to complete in the post. If your financial affairs are particularly complicated, then you may still be required to attend at the OR's office in person for one or more interviews.

If you were made bankrupt by a **creditor**, the OR's office will contact you to arrange an appointment to see the OR or a member of their staff. They will also send you some documents to complete as best you can before the appointment.

The OR is a civil servant. This is the person who administers and investigates your affairs in the early stages. When you go to the OR's office (or speak to staff on the telephone) you will be interviewed by one of their Examiners, who are also civil servants. The interview may take something over an hour, mostly devoted to completing more forms.

At the interview, the OR or one of their Examiners will:

o check that you have filled in the forms correctly;

o tell you the various things you cannot do as a bankrupt; and

o ask you to explain, in your own words, why you are in this situation.

The Examiner will take notes of the interview and you will be asked to sign them to confirm that the notes are accurate.

If you do not give the OR's office your full co-operation, then they can apply to court for your discharge from bankruptcy to be suspended until such time as you do co-operate.

It is also likely that you may find yourself subject to a **bankruptcy restriction order** (see below).

Banking considerations

Within a day or so of the bankruptcy order being made against you, the OR will close down all the bank accounts, etc in which you have an interest, including any joint accounts. The OR will take any money that remains in your accounts, although they may return some to cover household expenses.

It is vital, therefore, before the bankruptcy order is made, to make sure you are able to pay your essential household bills if these are normally paid by direct debit out of your bank account.

o   If you have wages that are shortly to be paid into your bank account, then you ought to make alternative arrangements with your employer; otherwise your wages may be paid into your bank account just before it is frozen. Arrange for your wages to be paid into the account of your partner (assuming the account is not in joint names, as that account will be frozen too!) or take your wages in cash.

o   Further, if you have a joint account with your partner, get them to remove your name from it at once to prevent it from being frozen.

o   If possible, also make sure all of your standing orders and direct debits for household expenses are transferred to another bank account in your partner's name.

If you have been unable to take these proactive steps, you will probably have to make separate arrangements for the payment of household bills for a month or so while a new bank account is being set up after the bankruptcy order has been made.

It is not illegal for a bankrupt to have a bank account; but when you open one you will need to tell the OR about it, so that they can keep a check on your income and also any other assets that may come to you after the bankruptcy order has been made.

In practice, you may find it more difficult to persuade a bank to give you an account. The British Bankers' Association produce a helpful leaflet (see 'Useful contacts'). Unfortunately, they do not actually list the banks offering services to bankrupts. The Bankruptcy Advisory Service used to produce a list of banks willing to open accounts for bankrupts, but this is no longer available.

If you surf the web using the key words 'bank account for bankrupts' you will be offered a great many sites. Websites change all the time, but we turned up 1,550 in January 2004. Beware! Many of these sites will charge for setting up an account for you. For example, www.creditsolutions.f9.co.uk lists possible accounts and a fee of £35 for setting one up for you. We're sure they'd do a good job, but is there any good reason why you could not DIY for free?

If you do have problems opening an account, then it may be worth speaking to the OR's Examiner who is dealing with your case, as a letter from them to the bank may help.

Notification

Your bankruptcy order will be advertised by the OR in the Public Notices section of the local newspaper, along with the planning and licensing applications. This kind of public humiliation can be prevented or postponed in only very limited circumstances, usually because the **bankruptcy order** should not have been made for some reason, or in exceptional circumstances.

You can find a typical Bankruptcy Notice on p 148.

If you think this applies to you, and you believe you ought never to have been bankrupted, seek legal advice. Quick, put this book down and get going!

Your duties

While you are bankrupt you owe various duties to the **OR**, principally to be absolutely honest and open with them about your assets and liabilities at the date of the **bankruptcy order**. You must also advise the OR of any changes in your financial circumstances (a change of job or maybe a lottery win?) until you are discharged.

You must:

o   hand over all books, papers and other records you have in your control or possession (this also includes certain privileged documents held by solicitors);

o   provide an inventory of your **assets**;

o   provide such further information as may be reasonably required; and

o   personally attend meetings with the OR or his staff when asked to do so.

It is a criminal offence to mislead the **OR** or to attempt to conceal facts from him. Such an offence is punishable by a fine or imprisonment. Please note that the courts often take the view that there is not much point fining somebody who is **bankrupt**, so the alternative of a prison sentence becomes more likely than it otherwise might have been.

Initially the OR is not your **Trustee in Bankruptcy** but a 'receiver and manager' of your **estate**. The OR has the power to sell any perishable goods, or goods that are likely to diminish in value in the short term, and protect all other assets that you owned at the date of the bankruptcy order. You are also required to ensure that all your assets are protected.

The OR, following completion of the forms referred to on p 95, will send a report to all your **creditors**, setting out the initial findings.

13

The Trustee in Bankruptcy and your assets

Enter the Trustee in Bankruptcy

Within 12 weeks of the date of your bankruptcy order the **Official Receiver** must decide whether or not to call a meeting of your **creditors** to seek the appointment of a **Licensed Insolvency Practitioner (LIP)** as your **Trustee in Bankruptcy (Trustee)**. If the Official Receiver decides to call such a meeting, the meeting must take place within four months of the bankruptcy order.

The main question the Official Receiver will consider is whether you have any **assets** that are worth realising; if you have 'realisable assets' likely to raise £5,000 or more, it is extremely likely that an LIP will be appointed (the reason being that the LIP will charge for their time and there needs to be enough money in the kitty to pay for this). If the Official Receiver decides not to call a meeting of creditors, they will send notice of this to all your creditors, at which point the Official Receiver will put on a new hat and become your Trustee in Bankruptcy.

If the Official Receiver decides to call a meeting, notice will be sent to all of your creditors, who will be entitled to vote for the appointment of any LIP they wish. The LIP with the highest number of votes (in value of money owed, as opposed to numbers of creditors) will be appointed as your Trustee. If no Trustee is appointed at the meeting, then each Official Receiver's office has a list of local LIPs called the rota. The rota is like a cab rank; the Official Receiver will simply appoint the LIP named at the top of the rota.

Unfortunately, if your creditors are principally credit card companies you may find that your Trustee in Bankruptcy may not be local to you and may be hundreds of miles away. However, if your Trustee wishes to see you, you should ask for your reasonable travel costs to be paid.

At any time after the bankruptcy order the Official Receiver may appoint an LIP as your Trustee in Bankruptcy whether or not the Official Receiver accepted the appointment as your Trustee (provided, of course, another Trustee has not been appointed already). This is known as a 'Secretary of State' appointment and is used in complicated or urgent cases, where a Trustee's appointment cannot wait for a creditors' meeting. The classic example is where an individual has gone bankrupt who owns and runs a nursing home. Clearly someone must take over the running of the business.

What do you get to keep?

The **Trustee in Bankruptcy** may be friendly and approachable (though a few are not), but remember that they are emphatically *not* on your side. Their role is to realise all of your **assets** at the best price possible for the benefit of your creditors.

The definition of 'assets' is extremely wide and includes anything that has, or may have, a value, including houses (see below), land, life insurance policies, endowment policies, claims (known as 'causes of action') that you have against third parties, cars and so on.

It is a common misconception that as soon as you are made bankrupt the Trustee in Bankruptcy will come along to your home and take absolutely everything that you own, including anything owned by your partner and children. Some Victorian novels major in harrowing scenes in which the heartless **bailiffs** strip the debtor's home and even take the children's toys. All that was based on truth. When Charles Dickens's father was made bankrupt, all Charles's belongings, even his little bed, were carried off to be sold. Nowadays most household items will be left untouched by the Trustee.

PERSONAL INSOLVENCY

All the property and **assets** you owned at the date of the **bankruptcy order** 'vest in' the Trustee in Bankruptcy (come under their control) as soon as the Trustee in Bankruptcy is appointed. All, that is, except the following:

○ such tools, books, vehicles and other items of equipment as are necessary to the bankrupt for use personally in their employment, business or vocation, otherwise known as 'tools of the trade';

○ such clothing, bedding, furniture, household equipment and provisions as are necessary for 'satisfying the basic domestic needs' of the bankrupt and their family;

○ income (see below).

'Excessive value'

There are, however, exceptions to this list.

If any item is of 'excessive value', then the **Trustee in Bankruptcy** is entitled to claim it, whereupon they will sell it and keep the money for the benefit of the creditors. The Trustee is, however, required to pay you enough money to buy a replacement that is not of 'excessive value'. Two examples:

○ At home you have an antique dining room table worth £10,000. Clearly this is of excessive value and therefore the Trustee in Bankruptcy will sell it and perhaps give you £200 to buy a replacement dining room table.

○ You are a self-employed electrician and drive around in a brand new £30,000 Mercedes van. Clearly you could drive around in a cheaper replacement.

However, it is all relative. It may be that you can persuade a Trustee that a brand new Mercedes car is a tool of the trade as you are a financial advisor for whom 'image' is necessary and important. Good luck ...!

Income

As a starting point, the **Trustee in Bankruptcy** is not entitled to your income. However, where your income exceeds what is known in the trade as the 'reasonable domestic needs' of you and your family, then the Trustee is entitled to a share of any income over and above this level. In practical terms, the Trustee in Bankruptcy will ask you to provide details of your income and expenditure. You may have already done this, because the Statement of Affairs you completed at the date of the **bankruptcy order** required you to confirm this. The level of income that is excluded is different for each and every family.

The Trustee in Bankruptcy will then tell you what sum they believe you can afford to pay each month, and it may be possible to negotiate this. If you and the Trustee cannot reach an agreement, the Trustee can apply for the court to decide what you should pay. This is known as an **income payments order** (IPO). The court can also order, if you are an employee, for the employer to pay the Trustee directly.

As and when your income changes, either upwards or downwards, the agreement with the Trustee in Bankruptcy or the IPO can be varied accordingly. You are, of course, required to keep the Trustee informed of any changes in your income.

If you are self-employed or paid, for example, commission only, then your income may fluctuate quite substantially. Nevertheless, a formula can be agreed or ordered by the court whereby a certain amount of your income will be paid to the Trustee.

The income payments order can be made for a period of up to three years and may therefore go beyond your **discharge** from bankruptcy. In particular, please note that even though, with effect from 1 April 2004, you are likely to be discharged from bankruptcy after one year, an IPO can still continue for three years!

A new procedure called an 'income payment agreement' is also available with effect from 1 April 2004. This seems to have the same effect as an IPO, but without involving the court. It, too, may last up to three years and continue in force after the date of discharge. It does not appear to have any material advantage over an IPO or informal agreement with the Official Receiver or Trustee in Bankruptcy. Time will tell.

Ongoing threats

Readers with a classical education will recall the sword of Damocles, hanging by a single hair over the poor guy's head. Something similar can happen to **bankrupts**.

If you obtain your discharge from bankruptcy but an **asset** has not been recovered or **realised** by the Trustee in Bankruptcy; then the fact that the asset has not been recovered or realised during the term of the bankruptcy does not mean that you've timed out and the asset is safe. The law says that ownership of the asset does *not* revert to the bankrupt, but instead remains vested in the Trustee. This means that, while you may be discharged from bankruptcy, there may still be assets that need to be dealt with by the Trustee. Read on.

Your home in danger

The classic example of an **asset** that the **Trustee in Bankruptcy** must **realise** is the **bankrupt's** home. It is quite usual for the Trustee to decide that, as there may be little or no equity in your home at the time the bankruptcy order is made – ie, there will not be much left over after the mortgage and other expenses have been paid – the Trustee will hang onto it until property prices rise. Fine – but just because you get discharged from your bankruptcy, that does not mean that the Trustee cannot come along at some later stage, when there may be some equity in the property (it may take several years, but Trustees have long memories) and sell it then. They can and do.

This problem has been the subject of much legal debate. There are currently more than 6,000 homes in the UK occupied by discharged bankrupts. These people were made bankrupt in the 1980s and 1990s, but their homes have yet to be sold. The recent increase in house prices has meant that houses that had no equity (which, you will recall, is the difference between the value of the property and the amount owed on it) in the 1980s and 1990s have considerable equity now.

Some people do not even realise that they no longer own their house, as they have not fully understood how bankruptcy works. They were **discharged** long ago and they are getting on with their lives, unaware that their home is still under threat. The fact that they have dutifully paid their mortgage all this time is no protection.

Use it or lose it

The government wanted to resolve this issue and on 1 April 2004 the law changed to prevent such long delays.

Under the new legislation, if you are the subject of a bankruptcy **petition** presented *after 1 April 2004*, then your 'principal residence' (law-speak for your family home) becomes subject to the 'use it or lose it' rule.

The 'use it or lose it' rule applies to an interest you may have in a 'dwelling house' (law-speak again: a flat counts as a dwelling house too) which at the date of the **bankruptcy order** was the sole or principal residence for you, your spouse or your former spouse. The **Trustee** still has the power to dispose of your home, but now there is a time limit. The clock starts ticking as soon as the **bankruptcy order** is made and the deadline is three years.

If, at the end of the three years, the Trustee has not dealt with the property, they have, in effect, timed out and the property will 're-vest in the bankrupt'. In other words, the property, together with any value it may have gained in the meantime, will be returned to the bankrupt and the Trustee will have no further claim on it.

The Trustee in Bankruptcy is required, in such circumstances, to give notice of the expiry of the three-year period, and the consequent re-vesting, to any interested parties. This, of course, includes the bankrupt – ie, you and anyone else with an interest in the property. It also includes the Land Registry.

The Land Registry is the Domesday Book for the 21st century. They hold the records of who owns what, and where. You can find out more about the Land Registry on their website: www.landreg.gov.uk.

If your property is registered with the Land Registry, then the Trustee in Bankruptcy will also notify them. If your property is unregistered, you will receive a certificate confirming the position. This is because the **Official Receiver** or Trustee will have almost immediately registered their interest in the property with the Land Registry when you were made bankrupt, in order to stop you from selling it and running off with the proceeds.

If, for any reason, a **bankrupt** has failed to disclose their interest in a property within three months of the bankruptcy order, the three-year period does not start until the Official Receiver or Trustee in Bankruptcy becomes aware of the property. Withholding information will not, therefore, help you! The Trustee may also be able to apply to the court to extend the three-year period in exceptional circumstances.

The Trustee in Bankruptcy is required to serve notice of their interest on the bankrupt, their spouse or their former spouse as soon as is reasonably practicable.

Within the three-year period, the Trustee in Bankruptcy must do one of the following:

o   realise their interest in the property (see below);

o   apply to the court for possession;

o   apply for a charging order; or

o   enter into an agreement with the bankrupt.

If the Trustee in Bankruptcy takes any of these steps within the three-year period, then the 'use it or lose it' rule does not apply. The Trustee could therefore issue possession proceedings as late as the day before the three-year period is up.

'Use it or lose it' for earlier bankruptcies

What is the situation if you had a bankruptcy **petition** presented prior to 1 April 2004; or you are one of the thousands of people made bankrupt in the 1980s and 1990s whose house has not yet been dealt with? The news is not encouraging. The three-year period will run from 1 April 2004 and therefore the Trustee in Bankruptcy will have until 31 March 2007 to deal with your property.

Low value homes

With effect from 1 April 2004, the **Trustee in Bankruptcy** cannot get a court order for possession, sale or charging order on your home if the value of the Trustee's interest in the property is below the prescribed limit. The prescribed limit is now £1,000.

How does the Trustee in Bankruptcy 'realise their interest' – ie, get the money out of it?

The Trustee looks at your property with a view to selling it, and can only take into consideration the value of your own interest in the property. In many cases, a property will be jointly owned by you and your partner and in this case the Trustee can claim only the value of *your* share.

Here's how it works:

o   When calculating your share, the Trustee in Bankruptcy will take into account any existing mortgages held over the property. What is left over – the equity – is what the Trustee is interested in.

o   If the property is jointly owned, then your co-owner will normally claim at least one-half of the equity in the property already – and therefore will only have to raise one-half of the equity in order to pay off the Trustee.

o   The Trustee cannot touch your co-owner's share (assuming, of course, that your co-owner is free from bankruptcy).

The Trustee in Bankruptcy will nevertheless be able to force the sale of your home, if necessary, to get at your share, even though they can only touch a half-share of the equity.

However, before doing so, it is the usual practice of the Trustee in Bankruptcy to approach the **bankrupt** with a view to asking whether the other co-owner (usually a partner, whether married or not) or perhaps any other third party, such as friends or family, can raise enough money to buy the Trustee out. If there is not much equity, this may be relatively easy to do, as well as a smart move.

If family and friends cannot help, the co-owner may be able to take out a further mortgage to buy out the Trustee's share.

In some cases, it is not immediately clear who owns what, as the property may not be owned on a simple 50/50 basis. It may be the case that a partner can lay claim to more of the equity because, for example, the **bankrupt** has borrowed further money for their business by way of a secured loan held over the property, or the partner has paid for substantial improvements to the property. This is a legal principle known as 'the equitable right of exoneration'. (There. Now you can bore people at parties!)

Allowances may be also be made if your partner paid the deposit on the property when it was first bought. If this is the case, then you need to seek legal advice, as the law in this area is complicated and beyond the scope of this book.

In summary:

o Just because the property may be registered in the sole name of the bankrupt, does not always mean that the Trustee in Bankruptcy is entitled to all the equity in the property.

o Conversely, just because the property is registered in the sole name of the non-bankrupt partner, doesn't mean the Trustee in Bankruptcy has no claim on the property.

o Just because the property is registered in the joint names of the bankrupt and their partner, does not mean that the equity is always split equally between the Trustee in Bankruptcy and the partner. 50/50 is just the starting point!

Can you buy the Trustee in Bankruptcy out while your home isn't worth much?

Suppose there was very little equity in your home at the time of your bankruptcy, and the **Trustee** has not sold the property for some time after the bankruptcy because there was little to gain from this, but the property market has been buoyant in the meantime.

Clearly, the more your home increases in value, the more money there is in it for the Trustee, and hence the more money that will need to be found to buy them out. Simply carrying on paying the mortgage also effectively makes your home worth more to the Trustee. However, if you do not continue to pay the mortgage, then the bank or building society may repossess your home anyway. This is a very common problem and creates a 'catch 22' situation, particularly in view of the way in which property values have increased over the last few years.

Remember: it works both ways. You may go bankrupt at a time when there is substantial equity in the property; and shortly thereafter the housing market collapses. This means the Trustee's interest in the property decreases as well.

It is worth remembering, therefore, that if you are made bankrupt at a time when there is little or no equity in your property, you may be able to buy the Trustee's interest for as little as £1 plus the Trustee's costs. If the **Official Receiver** is your Trustee in Bankruptcy, these costs are currently £211. If your Trustee in Bankruptcy is not the Official Receiver, then this figure will need to be negotiated with your Trustee, but it should still not be a fortune.

Whatever the value of the equity in your home, it may be possible to negotiate an agreement to purchase the Trustee's interest in the property. How is this done?

o   First of all, you will need to obtain a valuation of the property. It is advisable to get a proper valuation, undertaken by a surveyor (who is FRICS or ARICS qualified), rather than an estate agent. Whilst this will cost more (between £80 and £150) as opposed to an estate agent's valuation (which is usually free), a surveyor will give an opinion of the *true* value of the property whereas an estate agent may give the 'hopeful' value of the property. There is nothing to stop you from getting more than one valuation, as you only need to disclose the lowest valuation to the Trustee.

o   You will also need to ask the mortgage lender for an up-to-date balance on the mortgage, together with balances from anyone else who has security on the property.

- If you deduct these secured balances from the value of the property, this will give you an idea of the amount of equity you are dealing with.

- If you are going to make an offer to the Trustee in Bankruptcy, they should also allow for the reasonable *costs* of selling the property. Why? If you do not reach an agreement, the Trustee will repossess the property in due course and will also need to instruct estate agents and solicitors and, of course, pay their fees. Therefore, the estate agent's fees and solicitor's fees should be deducted from the equity. See the examples below.

Example

Value of house:	£120,000
Mortgage:	£100,000
Equity:	£20,000

If the property is registered in joint names with you and your partner having equal shares then, on the face of it, the Trustee's interest in the property is worth £10,000. However, the costs of sale have to be taken into account:

Equity	£20,000
Less estate agent's fees	
(say 2% plus VAT of £120,000)	– 2,820
Less solicitors costs	– 500
	———
Total equity available to Trustee: =	£16,680

The Trustee may therefore accept 50% of this figure, ie, £8,340.

Please note that this example is a straightforward one; if improvements have been made to the property by the non-bankrupt co-owner, or debts have been secured against the property in respect of your individual debts only, then the figures above may change completely. Seek legal advice!

Please note that someone other than the bankrupt should make this offer, unless the bankrupt has been discharged.

A legal agreement can be drawn up whereby the purchaser of the Trustee in Bankruptcy's interest will buy the property subject to the current mortgage, rather than having to take out a new mortgage with the accompanying expense. The Trustee will require their interest to be purchased by means of a lump sum payment, or possibly by instalments over a very short period of time.

Before anything of this kind can happen, the mortgage lender's consent will be needed. This is usually given if the purchaser can realistically take on the mortgage and meet the mortgage lender's conditions. If the mortgage lender will not agree, the transaction may still be possible, although it is beyond the scope of this book – once again, seek legal advice.

Endowment policies

Many home buyers take out an endowment policy when they take out their mortgage, to ensure that the mortgage is paid at the end of the term. If someone who is bankrupt has done the same, and if the endowment policy has been running for several years, then the chances are that it has a substantial surrender value. As the endowment policy is an **asset** in which the **Trustee in Bankruptcy** acquires an interest, they will want to **realise** their share (note that if the bankrupt took out the policy jointly with their partner only half the value will be available to the Trustee).

Again, the Trustee in Bankruptcy will approach the **bankrupt** to see whether or not any other person can buy out the bankrupt's share; but it can often be impossible for any third party to raise enough money to buy out the Trustee's share in both the property and the endowment policy.

Avoiding eviction

By this time, you will be viewing the **Trustee in Bankruptcy** as an ogre. The fact that the Trustee is there to get the best deal for your **creditors** and is only doing their job isn't much comfort. They say Attila the Hun was fond of little children ...! As we said above, if nobody can buy out the Trustee's interest, then the Trustee must look to sell your home and give the proceeds to the creditors.

The Trustee in Bankruptcy cannot simply do this on their own initiative. The Trustee has to apply to the court within three years of your bankruptcy order for an order to evict you and your family from the property so that it can be sold. You and any co-owners will receive notice of this application. The court is likely to grant the possession order unless you can show that you can purchase the Trustee's interest and/or the Trustee has not given you credit for, for example, improvements paid for by your partner. Again, you must seek legal advice if this happens.

Sorry to be flippant, but in some situations it pays to stay married. Certainly it pays to have children at home. Provided:

o   a husband or wife lives with you; and/or

o   there are children at home,

the property cannot be sold by the Trustee in Bankruptcy in the first year after the Trustee is appointed unless there are exceptional circumstances. This gives you some breathing space, at least.

Married or not, after the first year the Trustee in Bankruptcy is likely to be successful in obtaining possession and evicting you, unless exceptional circumstances exist. These exceptional circumstances are rare and usually apply where someone who lives in the property is extremely ill or very old.

In this situation, the **Trustee in Bankruptcy** might look to a charging order instead. The Trustee will ask the court to grant them security over the property by means of a **charge**. This will be similar to a mortgage and must be repaid when the property is sold. It will not be necessary to make any payments towards the charge until the property is sold.

The Trustee will usually instruct additional professionals to help, such as surveyors, solicitors and accountants. If, for example, one of the co-authors, Andrew McTear, were appointed your Trustee, you might hear from one of the other co-authors, Frank Brumby, as the solicitor who will advise the Trustee.

'Any dodgy transactions?'

Your home may be your biggest **asset**, but there are other assets to consider too.

The **Trustee in Bankruptcy** also has the power to go back certain periods of time and set aside or reverse certain transactions entered into by the bankrupt. These transactions, collectively known as **antecedent transactions**, are set out below.

Transactions at an undervalue

This applies for the period of five years before the date of the *presentation* of the **bankruptcy petition** (this is the date the petition is **filed** with the court, either by the **creditor** or the **debtor**).

Where the **bankrupt** has transferred or sold **assets** (which includes money as well!) either by way of a gift (such as giving your son your expensive sports car) or at a significant discount (such as selling your Cartier watch to your best friend for £10), then the **Trustee in Bankruptcy** has the power to issue proceedings against the person *who received* the asset and ask the court to restore the position. Usually the person who received the asset cheaply or as a gift will be ordered by the court to pay the sum they should have paid for the gift/asset; for example, if the Cartier watch was worth £5,000, the best friend would be required to pay £4,990 (see also the Purdey shotgun example in 'FAQs').

If the transaction took place between two and five years prior to the presentation of the bankruptcy petition, rather than during the two years immediately before the petition, then the Trustee in Bankruptcy must also establish that the person who gave the assets/gift away (the future bankrupt):

- ○ was insolvent at the time; *or*
- ○ became insolvent as a result of giving the asset/gift away.

If the person receiving the asset/gift is related to the giver (known as an 'associate'), the court will assume that the future bankrupt was insolvent at the time. It will be for the person defending the proceedings to prove that the future bankrupt was not insolvent at the time. It is irrelevant whether the person who received the assets knew about the insolvency.

Don't try to be clever – I

Don't think that you can outwit the **Trustee in Bankruptcy** by giving all your **assets** away before going **bankrupt**. This will simply mean that the person who benefited will have a Trustee knocking at their door at some point in the future, asking for some money, plus a further sum to cover the Trustee's costs! Furthermore, if it can be shown that you did it intentionally, you may find yourself the subject of a criminal prosecution. Note that you may also find yourself subject to a **bankruptcy restriction order** (see below).

Transactions defrauding creditors

These are transactions at undervalue, as above, except that there is no time limit. That is, the **Trustee in Bankruptcy** can try to set aside or reverse transactions that were entered into, for example, 20 years before the presentation of the bankruptcy **petition**. The Trustee will need to prove that the future **bankrupt** entered into the transaction with the prime purpose of putting **assets** beyond the reach of **creditors**.

Preferences

This applies for the period of:

- ○ six months prior to the date of the *presentation* of the **bankruptcy petition** if a third party is involved; or
- ○ two years if a family member is involved.

If, during this time, the **debtor** pays one **creditor** to the detriment of another, the **Trustee in Bankruptcy** can knock on the door of the creditor who was given preferential treatment and ask them to pay the money back. For example:

> Assume that Mr Toad has two creditors, Rat and Mole, each of whom is owed £1,000. Toad has £1,000; he pays Rat in full but pays nothing to Mole. The Trustee in Bankruptcy can sue Rat for the return of the money. If the debtor had paid Rat and Mole £500 each, then the Trustee could do nothing, as neither creditor had been *preferred*.

In this example, the Trustee in Bankruptcy will need to prove not only that Mr Toad was insolvent at the time, but also that it was Mr Toad's intention or desire to 'prefer' Rat to Mole so that Rat would be better off if Mr Toad went bankrupt. If the preferential treatment is with a family member, it is presumed by the court that Mr Toad had this desire or intention. The Trustee in Bankruptcy must therefore prove, in either event, that Mr Toad was insolvent at the time.

Don't try to be clever – 2

Suppose that you are going bankrupt and you want to make sure that your dear old mother, who previously loaned you some money, gets paid off. Unless you attend to another liability at the same time, such as reducing your credit card debt, the Trustee in Bankruptcy will come knocking at your mother's door and ask her to pay back the money – and their costs as well. Note, too, that you may also find yourself subject to a **bankruptcy restriction order**.

Extortionate credit transactions

If, before being made bankrupt, the **bankrupt** obtained credit for which they were charged a very high rate of interest at any time in the three-year period prior to bankruptcy, the **Trustee in Bankruptcy** may issue proceedings against the credit provider, requiring certain payments to be made to the Trustee.

What is an extortionate transaction? It is a transaction with grossly exorbitant payments or a transaction contravening ordinary principles of fair dealing. Please note, however, that it has been held that 50% APR was not extortionate in the circumstances of one particular transaction. This loan was extremely high-risk and therefore it was held by the court that the credit provider was entitled to a high return on this risky venture.

It is, however, quite rare for a Trustee in Bankruptcy to consider one of these claims.

Property acquired after bankruptcy

The **Trustee in Bankruptcy** is also entitled to everything in the way of **assets** that comes to you during the period of bankruptcy – ie, from the date of the bankruptcy order to the date of your **discharge**. These are called **after acquired assets** or property. Any legacies, windfalls or lottery wins would come into this category (see below).

If you do acquire any assets of value (by whatever means), then you are required to notify your Trustee in Bankruptcy within 21 days. This includes any increase in your income. The Trustee then has 42 days from your notice to confirm whether or not they are claiming the asset. It is extremely likely that the Trustee will claim the asset. They will then sell it for the benefit of the **creditors**.

Once again, if you do not disclose this, you may be committing a criminal offence (see 'Interlude: practical matters', p 91). This issue used to crop up regularly. However, post-1 April 2004, the period in which property can be acquired is much shorter, reduced from three years to less than one year, so this should be less of a problem.

Pensions

The law relating to pensions has seen a great deal of change recently. If your **bankruptcy petition** was **presented** before 29 May 2000, then as the law currently stands your pension policy will belong to the **Trustee in Bankruptcy**, who will be entitled to receive the benefits you would have received, in other words the lump sum and the income (annuity) for the remainder of your life. This applies both to private pension schemes and occupational pension schemes, although you will be entitled to the 'protected rights' element of the pension, which equates to the national minimum pension.

Please note that some pension policies have forfeiture clauses that *may* operate to your advantage in the event of bankruptcy so that the Trustee in Bankruptcy is not entitled to the benefits. If you feel this might be the case, you should seek legal advice.

The good news is that if your bankruptcy petition was presented on or after 29 May 2000, your pension policy, provided it is 'approved' by the Inland Revenue, does *not* belong to the Trustee in Bankruptcy – ie, it remains your pension policy and the Trustee cannot realise it for the benefit of **creditors**. Basically, any pension policy that benefits from Inland Revenue exemptions (probably all but a few 'self-administered' pensions funds) will be approved.

If you elect to benefit from your pension before you are **discharged** from bankruptcy, the Trustee in Bankruptcy can 'attack' any lump sum as an **after acquired asset** and will take into account your annuity as part of your income. If possible, therefore, it is wise not to do anything with your pension until after you have been discharged from bankruptcy, as any money you get as a result of electing to take your pension during the bankruptcy will be seen as an **asset** and can be claimed by the Trustee in Bankruptcy.

Furthermore, it should be noted that a Trustee in Bankruptcy could also attack payment of any excessive contributions you have made into your pension fund either prior to the bankruptcy or during it. This is still a relatively new law and at this time there have been no cases decided by the courts on the point as to what is classed as being 'excessive'. But a much larger payment than in previous years might be risky.

What happens to the money the Trustee in Bankruptcy receives from the sale of assets?

The **Trustee in Bankruptcy** is required to distribute the money in accordance with the law. Known **creditors** will be invited to lodge with the Trustee a 'proof of debt' form together with evidence of their claim. The Trustee in Bankruptcy will also advertise in local newspapers for any other creditors to lodge their claims, giving them a deadline to do so.

The Trustee will then go through the process of accepting or rejecting, wholly or in part, the claims of the creditors. You might be required to assist with that process. If the Trustee rejects any part of a creditor's claim, the Trustee must give written notice of their reasons for doing so. If the creditor does not agree with the Trustee's decision, the creditor will have 21 days in which to apply to court, at which point the court will determine the correct amount to be claimed.

The queue

If you are particularly unhappy with a Trustee's decision (such as because they may have admitted a claim which you do not think is due), then you can also apply to court.

Once all of the claims have been agreed, the **Trustee in Bankruptcy** will make payments to creditors, known as a **dividend**. First in the queue are any secured creditors. Once the **assets** have been sold, each will be paid from the sale proceeds of the particular asset over which they have security. If the secured creditor still has money owing to them, this balance will be an unsecured debt.

Next the **preferential creditors** will be paid. The definition of a preferential creditor depends on when your **bankruptcy petition** was presented. If it was presented *before 15 September 2003*, then the preferential creditors that you need to know about are:

o   Inland Revenue, for any PAYE and/or National Insurance deducted from employees in the 12-month period prior to the bankruptcy order;

o   HM Customs & Excise, for any unpaid VAT in the six-month period prior to the bankruptcy order;

o   any unpaid holiday pay;

o   any unpaid wages up to £800 in the four-month period prior to the **bankruptcy order**.

If your petition was presented *on or after 15 September 2003*, then the only preferential creditors are employees. The **Crown debts** (ie, to the Revenue and HM Customs & Excise) are now unsecured.

Each of the preferential creditors will be paid the same proportion of their debt, ie, 25 pence in the pound means they will all get 25% of the debt paid in full. Only if they are paid 100% (and there is some money left in the kitty!) do the next **creditors** in the queue receive a payment. These are the unsecured creditors and will form the main bulk of your debt. If and when these creditors are paid in full, the last person on the list is your husband or wife, who is right at the back of the queue and does not get a penny until everyone else has been paid off!

16

Bankruptcy cramps your style

There are a number of restrictions on **bankrupts**, and you would commit a criminal offence if you **breached** them. It is a criminal offence, among other things, for you:

o   to obtain credit (goods, cash or services) over £500 (either on your own or with anyone else) without first disclosing to the person from whom you are obtaining credit that you are a bankrupt;

o   to fail to disclose details of all of your property to the **Official Receiver (OR)** or **Trustee in Bankruptcy** or fail to disclose details of any transactions previously entered into that could be attacked as **antecedent transactions** (see above);

o   to conceal property (or books or papers) or fail to deliver up property when requested to do so by the OR or Trustee;

o   to make false statements or material omissions;

o   to dispose of property fraudulently;

o   to leave or attempt to leave (or make preparations to leave) England and Wales with any property worth more than £1,000 to which the Trustee is entitled;

o   to dispose of property purchased on credit that has not been paid for in the 12 months prior to bankruptcy;

o   to trade in a name which is not a name in which you were made bankrupt, unless you tell the supplier or customer you are a bankrupt; or

o   to be, or act in any way as if you are, a company director or be involved directly or indirectly in the formation, promotion or management of a company. Do not try to be clever; do not name your partner (married or not) as a director and then manage the business yourself in the background. Any person who acts on the instructions of a bankrupt in relation to a company may be *personally* liable for all of the company's debts.

The table below sets out these offences. The left hand column refers to the section of the Insolvency Act 1986 as amended by the Enterprise Act 2002.

The Enterprise Act 2002 'demoted' two offences. These are

o   rash hazardous spending (which would now only earn you a **bankruptcy restriction order (BRO)**) and

o   failing to keep adequate records (another BRO offence).

In 2002/03, 44 people were convicted of obtaining credit while a **bankrupt** and 158 were convicted of other bankruptcy offences.

The bankruptcy restriction order

Before the Enterprise Act 2002 came into force, all **bankrupts** were treated the same, regardless of whether they were actively dodgy or honest but ill-advised. This was hard on the latter, but let the former off lightly.

With effect from 1 April 2004, a new regime begins. The 'honest failures' will normally be **discharged** within 12 months. The dodgy ones may find themselves subject to a **BRO**. This is a regime that mirrors very closely the disqualification of rogue directors of limited companies already in force.

When the OR investigates your affairs, they may report your conduct (both before and after the bankruptcy order) to the Department of Trade and Industry (DTI). If the DTI is dissatisfied with your conduct, proceedings will be issued against you; and the court will be asked to take into account various matters, including:

- failing to keep records which account for a loss of property or by a business carried on by you in the two-year period prior to the bankruptcy **petition** date;
- failing to produce records of that kind on demand by the OR;
- entering into a transaction at an undervalue;
- giving a preference;
- making an excessive pension contribution;
- failing to supply goods or services that were wholly or partly paid for;
- trading at a time when you knew or ought to have known you were unable to pay your debts;
- incurring a debt that you had no reasonable expectation of being able to repay;
- failing to account satisfactorily for loss of property;
- gambling or rash hazardous spending that has contributed materially to the bankruptcy debts;
- neglecting business affairs which has contributed to the bankruptcy debts;
- fraud or fraudulent breach of trust;
- failing to co-operate with the OR and/or Trustee;
- whether or not this is the second bankruptcy in the previous six years.

The application for a BRO must be started by the DTI within one year of the **bankruptcy order**, unless the court gives permission to issue at a later date. The BRO can remain in force for a period of between two and 15 years, depending on how badly you have behaved.

As an alternative to a court application for a BRO, a bankrupt can also give an undertaking (ie, a solemn promise) to the court. This is called a 'bankruptcy restriction undertaking' (BRU) and is a quicker and less costly procedure than a BRO. If the bankruptcy order is annulled, then in limited circumstances, the BRO or BRU will no longer have effect either.

Bankruptcy offences

BANKRUPTCY OFFENCES*

SECTION*	OFFENCE	DEFENCE	PENALTY
353	Non disclosure to the OR/Trustee of any property comprised in the bankrupt's estate and/or fails to disclose any disposal of assets which may be capable of setting aside		7 years imprisonment, fine or both
354 (1) and (2)	If the debtor fails to deliver to the OR all or any of his assets or if he conceals any debt due to or from him with a greater value than £1,000. Applies retrospectively to period of 12 months prior to bankruptcy petition	Innocent intention (s.352)	
355	Bankrupt fails to deliver up books, papers, and other records and/or prevents production, conceals, or destroy the records. Applies retrospectively to period of 12 months prior to bankruptcy petition		
356	Bankrupt makes false statement or made any material omission		
359	Bankrupt disposes of any property obtained on credit in respect of which money still owing in period of 12 months prior to bankruptcy petition		
357	Bankrupt transfers any property or makes a gift at any time within 5 years prior to the bankruptcy petition. Also offence if debtor conceals or removes property within 2 months before or after a county court judgment has been obtained against him		
358	Bankrupt leaves or attempts to leave or makes any preparation to leave England/Wales with property valued at more than £1,000 in 6 months prior to bankruptcy petition	No defence	2 years imprisonment of a fine or both
360	Bankrupt obtains credit either solely or jointly with another in excess of £500 without informing the creditor that he is a bankrupt. Wide definition of credit!		
354(3)	Bankrupt fails to account for loss of any substantial part of his property incurred in the 12 months before bankruptcy petition		
11 (CDDA 1986)	Bankrupt is directly or indirectly involved in the management of a limited company without leave of the court		

* Up to date as at 1st April 2004 incorporating Enterprise Act 2002 and Insolvency Proceedings (Monetary Limits)(Amendment) Order 2003

What does a BRO or BRU do?

A **BRO** or BRU continues the restrictions of bankruptcy for whatever period the BRO or BRU states – that is, you cannot incur credit of more than £500 without disclosing that you are bankrupt; you can only trade in your own name (or the name in which you were made bankrupt) or be involved in a limited company. Neither can you practise certain professions, including that of **Licensed Insolvency Practitioner** (which makes sense!).

Whilst it is too early to say, the government believes that the BRO regime is likely to affect about 10% of bankrupts.

17

Free at last?

Escape routes

There are two main ways of escaping the bankruptcy regime: annulment and an **individual voluntary arrangement (IVA)**.

I Annulment

A **bankruptcy order** can be annulled at any time and there are two grounds for annulment:

(a) the bankruptcy debts and costs have been paid in full; *or*

(b) the bankruptcy order should never have been made in the first place.

We will deal with each of these in turn.

(a) I have the money ...

It is fair to say that most bankruptcies result in the **creditors** receiving a small dividend, ie, x pence for each pound they are owed. But suppose you are like Mr Micawber and something turns up.

If at any time during your bankruptcy period you are able to show that:

o all the creditors have been paid in full; *and*

o the **Trustee's** fees have been paid, as have the costs and expenses of the bankruptcy; *and*

o the creditors have received interest on their debts,

you can then apply for an annulment of your bankruptcy order. This is not as simple as it sounds, however.

For example, let us assume you went bankrupt owing £50,000 to creditors. To get an annulment you will need to pay this back in full. You will also need to pay the **Official Receiver's** costs and **disbursements** (which may be as much as £1,000) and the Trustee's costs which, depending upon the complexity of the case and the assets realised, could be as much as £10,000 or more. If you have sufficient **assets**, creditors are also entitled to statutory interest at the rate of 8% per annum. This interest ticks up like a taxi meter from the date of the bankruptcy order to the date of payment. So if you went bankrupt on 1 January 2000 for £50,000 and paid everyone on 1 January 2005, there will be 5 years' interest to pay on the £50,000 – a swingeing £20,000.

Finally there is the 'DTI fee'. All money received by a Trustee in Bankruptcy must be paid into the Insolvency Services Account. A percentage of all the money paid into this account is taken by the DTI (Department of Trade and Industry), starting at a rate of 15%, or 17% from 1 April 2004.

From this example, you will have calculated that you need to pay the following:

Creditors	£50,000
Interest	£20,000
OR's costs	£1,000
Trustee's Costs	£10,000
Total	£81,000

As this sum will be paid to the Trustee in Bankruptcy, who will then pay it into the Insolvency Services Account, the figure of £81,000 will need to be grossed up by 15%. You will need to pay £93,150 – nearly twice the original debt.

It is very expensive to get out of bankruptcy! The authors regularly come across individuals who simply ignore their problems and are made bankrupt for very small sums, but who may have considerable assets. Be warned!

There are legitimate ways of avoiding some of these fees, ways which may save thousands of pounds. They are beyond the scope of this book, however, and you should seek professional insolvency advice.

The effect of an annulment is to put the clock back, and to put you back to where you were before the bankruptcy order was made. All assets that have not been sold by the Trustee in Bankruptcy are returned to you, and the Trustee in Bankruptcy can no longer have any claim over them. You have, however, lost all the assets the Trustee in Bankruptcy has sold in the meantime: unscrambling omelettes isn't humanly possible.

(b) If it was all a dreadful mistake …

If the bankruptcy order should never have been made in the first place, ie, you didn't owe the creditor the debt after all, then you can also apply to annul the bankruptcy order. If this applies to you, you must move fast. The longer you leave it, the less likely you are to get your bankruptcy annulled. If you think it applies to you, check out the leaflet *Can My Bankruptcy Be Cancelled?* on the Insolvency Service website www.insolvency.gov.uk/guidanceleaflets/guides.htm (see 'Useful contacts' for details).

Although this might seem strange, it is also possible to have your bankruptcy order annulled *after* you have been discharged. The main reason to consider this is that the bankruptcy order, even after you have been discharged, will remain on your credit history for up to six years. If the bankruptcy order is annulled, it can be removed from your credit history altogether!

If your **bankruptcy order** is annulled for any reason, send a copy of the relevant court order to the credit reference agencies who will then remove the bankruptcy details from your credit history.

---

2 IVAs for bankrupts

Strangely, a bankrupt can propose an **IVA**, provided they have not yet been **discharged**. This happens more often than you might think. Many people are made bankrupt, not realising that they could have proposed an IVA to their creditors. If the IVA is approved, the bankruptcy order can be annulled as well.

Proposing an IVA is one such way of reducing the fees referred to in the example above, as an IVA avoids the fees that would otherwise have to be paid into the Insolvency Services Account. This would give you an immediate saving of £12,150 on the figures above!

You may either approach your **Trustee in Bankruptcy** asking them to agree to be your **nominee** or, alternatively, approach another **Licensed Insolvency Practitioner**. The procedure is the same as the one set out in the IVA section of this book (see Chapter 10). The only difference is that the **Official Receiver** and the Trustee in Bankruptcy (if the Trustee is not your nominee) is also served with the court documents, giving them an opportunity to object to your Proposal. They are not likely to object, as long as you have co-operated with them. Lastly, the IVA will need to provide for the costs of the Official Receiver and Trustee in Bankruptcy to be paid in full.

This approach is only useful if there are substantial assets to sell.

Fast-track IVAs

With effect from 1 April 2004, a new form of IVA is available exclusively for undischarged bankrupts. The buzzword is 'Fast-track IVAs' and the **Official Receiver** will be both **nominee** and **Supervisor**.

In brief, the Official Receiver will circulate a **Proposal** to creditors inviting them to approve it. There will be no creditors' meeting and no facility for the creditors to put forward modifications. If the IVA is approved, the bankrupt can apply for an annulment of the **bankruptcy order**.

Free at last? – discharge from bankruptcy

With the new legislation, this becomes somewhat complicated during the transitional period:

o   If you are made bankrupt *after 1 April 2004* then you will be discharged after 12 months. The **Official Receiver**, however, may **file** a notice before then at court stating that the investigation of your affairs is unnecessary or has been concluded, in which case you may be discharged earlier, on the date of the filing of the notice.

o   If you were made bankrupt *before 1 April 2004* then you will be **discharged** *either* on the expiry of three years from your bankruptcy order *or* 1 April 2005, whichever is the earlier date.

For example, if you were made bankrupt on 30 November 2003, you will be discharged on 1 April 2005. If you were made bankrupt on 2 February 2002, you will be discharged on 2 February 2005.

But if you fail to comply with your obligations to the Official Receiver or Trustee, then the period can be extended by an application to court:

o   If you are currently bankrupt for the second time, having been made bankrupt at any time in the previous 15 years, then you will not be discharged until the period of five years minimum from the date of the most recent **bankruptcy order**.

o   If you jumped – presented your own bankruptcy **petition** *prior to 1 April 2004 – and* your debts were less than £20,000, the court may have made an order of summary administration, in which case you will be discharged *either* on the expiry of two years *or* on 1 April 2005, whichever is earlier.

Note: there will be no such thing as 'summary administration' (ie, the two-year bankruptcy period for people whose total indebtedness is £20,000 or less) from 1 April 2004.

The court will not tell you that you are discharged, nor will the Trustee in Bankruptcy (but see below). You must make a diary note of the date that you are made bankrupt so that you know when you have been discharged. Discharge is automatic – no application to court is required unless it is your second (or more) bankruptcy. In that case you must apply to the court for discharge. This application cannot be made – at least not successfully! – until five years after your most recent bankruptcy order.

If, on or after the date of discharge, you require, for whatever reason, proof that you have been discharged, there is a procedure to obtain a Certificate of Discharge. This is a piece of paper with the court seal on it certifying that you have been discharged from bankruptcy.

You need only write to the court, stating your full name, address and bankruptcy court number (this will be on the bankruptcy order or on any correspondence you received from the Official Receiver if you have kept it!) requesting a Certificate of Discharge, and enclosing the court fee of £60 – make your cheque out to HMPG (Her Majesty's Paymaster General).

A Certificate of Discharge is often handy to have if, for example, you are trying to buy anything on credit. The credit providers will undertake a credit search against you before offering credit and the fact that you have been made the subject of a **bankruptcy order** will appear on the search report. The fact that you have been discharged will not appear; and the easiest way to prove that you are no longer bankrupt is to produce a Certificate of Discharge.

As regards the Trustee in Bankruptcy, they may write to you (even when you have not yet been discharged) confirming they have applied, or will be applying, for release as your Trustee. This will usually be on the grounds that the Trustee has realised all the **assets** they can – but *what it does not mean is that you have necessarily been discharged early from your bankruptcy*. The Trustee in Bankruptcy will simply ride off into the sunset and instead the Official Receiver will become the Trustee in Bankruptcy until you have served your time.

The Trustee in Bankruptcy may, in certain circumstances, make an application to the court to suspend (law-speak for delay) your discharge, but will only do this if they believe, for example, that:

o   you have failed to explain matters properly to the Trustee; or o   you have failed properly to co-operate with the Trustee.

You will, of course, be given an opportunity to attend the court to answer the Trustee's allegations.

A clean slate?

Discharge releases you from all 'provable debts' in the bankruptcy (*but* see p 105 about your home). The only debts that are not 'provable' in bankruptcy are:

o   criminal fines;

o   arrears of maintenance payments due under family court orders; and

o   any debts incurred by fraudulent conduct.

Certainly debts to the Inland Revenue, HM Customs & Excise, credit card companies, trade creditors, etc are all wiped out by the bankruptcy.

Debts to councils

The legal and practical position relating to council tax/business rates debts due under Liability Orders is not absolutely clear. Generally the view is that because a Liability Order has been made, the debt in question is not 'provable' (in this context – able to be wiped out) in the bankruptcy and therefore you will still remain liable, even when a **bankruptcy order** has been made and even when you have served your time and been discharged. If you have any debts due under Liability Orders in either of these respects, the legal position, therefore, is that you will remain liable to pay, and may be imprisoned for non-payment.

In practice, however, most local councils appear to take the view that as soon as a bankruptcy order has been made, the council will agree to 'participate in the bankruptcy'. On this basis, in practical terms you will not have to pay the debt.

We cannot know what attitude your local council takes towards bankrupts with Liability Orders against them. What is more, councils can change their policy. There is nothing to prevent a council that currently participates in bankruptcies in relation to council tax arrears from changing their policy at some stage.

Student loans

If you are thinking of going bankrupt to avoid paying off a student loan, have a care! As the law stands, if you have a student loan outstanding, it may not be provable in the bankruptcy – ie, you will still be liable for it after discharge. It depends upon when you received your student loan. If in doubt, take advice.

Afterword

A word of encouragement

All insolvencies cause a lot of stress to the people involved. The most anxious time will be the months leading up to the actual insolvency, and many people feel a great sense of relief once responsibility for their affairs has been passed to a **Licensed Insolvency Practitioner**.

One emotion that is not constructive is shame. The days of debtors' prisons are long past. As we said earlier, it is now accepted that in a dynamic market economy it is in the nature of risk-taking that we can't all be successful. The UK is moving towards the USA market where risk-taking and honest failure are acceptable elements of the enterprise economy. We mentioned 'honest failure' before. We repeat: the government has recognised that trying and failing in business, far from being a hanging offence, is a fundamental part of a dynamic market economy. Not trying is far more shameful than having a go and coming unstuck.

In the same way, in a society where credit is so easy to get, and the pressures to overspend are so great, small-time individual debtors can be excused a few indiscretions. We must not take sides here, but what about all the lenders who seem hell-bent on offering huge amounts of credit to complete strangers?

Just before we went to press, Rosy's little dog Gussie received a letter inviting 'Ms Gussie Rabson' to take out a credit card. How she got on the mailing list is a mystery!

'It's not the end of the world' is a very glib thing to say, especially to someone whose home is at risk. But there is life after insolvency. In fiction, something did finally turn up for Mr Micawber; and young Tom Tulliver paid his father's business debts in full. In real life, too, there are bound to be people near you who have survived financial ruin and gone on to rebuild their lives.

Insolvency can happen to anyone, rich and successful or poor and struggling, feckless and extravagant or just plain unlucky. Henry was a Lloyd's name who, through no fault of his own (except being badly advised), was stripped of literally everything he owned and brought to the brink of bankruptcy. It took this man several years to get on his feet again, but he did it. And he led an action group that successfully sued those whose bad advice had caused so much hardship.

Then there was Sharon, a young mother on state benefits who felt depressed and turned to 'retail therapy', all on credit, instead of to her doctor. Sharon came into a solicitor's office with a thick wad of court summonses and signed a form for free advice and assistance. Her solicitor negotiated an informal arrangement with the creditors and watched Sharon cut up all her cards. Sharon learned her lesson and is now an adviser in a Citizens Advice Bureau office.

If insolvency is staring you in the face, don't turn your back on it; it will only bite you in the bum. Face facts. As we said earlier:

- take control;
- be proactive;
- take advice; and then
- be positive about what you do next.

Good luck.

Letters and forms

Forms

All the forms you are ever likely to need are available on either the Insolvency Service website www.insolvency.gov.uk or the Court Service website: www.courtservice.gov.uk.

Draft letter to creditors

Here is a sample of the kind of letter you might send to a **creditor** if you were in financial difficulties. Naturally you will wish to vary it to meet your own needs, but the points you must include are:

o account number or other reference (even the smallest organisation seems to be computerised nowadays);

o balance outstanding;

o schedule of income and outgoings;

o schedule of assets (if any).

Dear

My Financial Affairs
Account Number/Reference:

I am writing in connection with my account with you, and I believe that there is a current balance outstanding of £*****. I am writing similarly to all of my creditors and I enclose a full list of all those of whom I am aware and to whom I have written.

Regrettably, my financial position is such that I am unable to afford to make the payments due and owing to my creditors. *[You need to go into more detail here – say in particular whether there has been any change in your circumstances, eg, loss of work, illness etc which has made it difficult for you to meet your liabilities].* I have no assets *[obviously, if you do have assets you will add 'apart from those listed on the attached schedule']* and am anxious to try to come to terms with my creditors.

I attach a schedule showing my current income and expenditure. As you can see, I have only a small surplus, ie, £***** after I have paid all my essential outgoings. Obviously, I do not have enough money left over to allow me to make all the payments required by my various creditors and I am therefore writing to make a proposal.

What I propose is that I will make available all of my surplus income, namely £******, to be distributed amongst all of my creditors on a monthly basis. *(An example of how to calculate this is described under the section headed 'Informal agreement'.)* In calculating the amount to be paid to each individual creditor I have taken into account the amounts owed and I propose to distribute on a *pro rata* basis. I have worked out how much each creditor will be entitled to receive and have listed the payments on the list of creditors. You will be entitled to receive £**** per month.

I propose to make this payment to you on a monthly basis until I have cleared my debt to you. Of course, if my financial position improves I shall try to increase the payments and shall advise you if this is the case.

For this proposal to be successful, I must have confirmation from each and every creditor that they are prepared to accept my terms, as I am aware that I must treat all creditors equally.

[Alternatively you can limit the period by saying:]

[I propose that I shall make these payments to you, on a monthly basis, for a period of three (see note below) years; and that you will accept the money which you receive during this period in full and final settlement of my liability to you. I say three years, as this is the maximum period of time for which I would be required to pay a proportion of my income if I was bankrupt under an income payments order.

If my circumstances change so as to allow me to increase my payments to creditors then I shall tell you with a view to increasing the instalments.]

Are you prepared to accept this proposal? Unfortunately, unless all my creditors are prepared to accept it, then I believe that I shall have no option but to consider bankruptcy. I would of course prefer to avoid bankruptcy, because I wish to pay my creditors as much as possible. I would be grateful, therefore, if you would seriously consider this proposal and kindly let me know within the next 14 days whether or not you are prepared to accept.

I look forward to hearing from you.

It may be that you have limited debts and, as you may only be **bankrupt** for one year, you should not propose to continue making payments for too long. If you have been bankrupt before then, of course, there would be no automatic discharge after one year. If this is the case, then you should obtain professional advice before writing to your **creditors**.

Statement of income and expenditure

This Statement of Income and Expenditure has three functions.

1. It provides the necessary headings for that rigorous overhaul of your personal finances before you decide what to do next.

2. If you decide to offer your **creditors** an informal arrangement, this statement can give your creditors the information they need to evaluate your **Proposal**. Enclose it with your letter (see p 140).

3. If you decide to seek a professional's advice, the same statement will save time and help your adviser to get to grips with your problems.

Statement of Income and Expenditure

1   PERSONAL DETAILS

Debtor's name ....

Address ....

Telephone .... (day) .... (evening)

Age ....

Status: married/cohabiting/single/other (please specify) ....

Number of children .... Ages of children ....

Other dependants ....

2   EMPLOYMENT STATUS

2.1   Employed

Employer's name ....

Employer's address ....

Job title ....

Annual wage or salary ....

2.2   Self-employed

Name of business ....

Business address ....

Nature of business ....

Annual earnings ....

2.3   Unemployed

Nature of last job ....

Length of time out of work ....

2.4 Pension

Name of pension provider(s) ....

Annual amount of pension(s) ....

2.5 Other ....

3 ASSETS

3.1 Home

Do you own your own home? Yes/No
If yes:

      Are you the sole owner? or co-owner? ....

      Value of home ....

      Amount of mortgage ....

      Name of mortgage lender ....

3.2 Vehicles

Do you own a car or other motor vehicles? Yes/No
If yes, please complete the following details for each vehicle you own:

      Make ....

      Registration no. ....

      Is vehicle on finance? Yes/No

      If yes, please give details in section 4, below.

3.3 Bank details

Do you have a bank account? Yes/No
If yes, please complete the following details for each account:

	1	2
Bank name		
Bank address		
Account name		
Account number		
Balance		

3.4 Savings and investments

Do you have any savings or investments? Yes/No
If yes, please provide details including value ....
....

3.5 Property

Do you own property other than your home? Yes/No
If yes, please provide the following details for each property:

	1	2
Are you the sole owner or co-owner?		
Value of home		
Amount of mortgage (if any)		
Name of mortgage lender		

3.6 Pensions

Do you or your employer pay into a pension scheme? Yes/No

If yes, please give details ....

Do you receive income from a pension which you have not

declared at 2.4? If so, please give details here ....

3.7 Other assets

Please provide details of any other assets you own, eg, boats,

jewellery, works of art etc. ....

....

3.8 Money owed to you

Does anybody owe you money? Yes/No

If yes, please give details of the debtor(s) and amount(s)

	1	2	3
Debtor			
Amount			

4 LIABILITIES

Please give details of money you owe, for example:

4.1 Credit card debts

	1	2	3
Name and address of lender			
Amount owed			
Monthly instalment			

4.2 Hire-purchase

(please complete for each hire-purchase arrangement you have)

	1	2	3
Name and address of lender			
Amount owed			
Monthly instalment			

4.3 Finance on vehicles
(please complete for each vehicle subject to finance)

	1	2	3
Name and address of lender			
Amount owed			
Monthly instalment			

4.4 Catalogue debts
(please complete for each debt)

	1	2	3
Lender			
Amount owed			
Weekly/monthly instalment			

4.5 County court judgments
(please complete for each judgment)

	1	2	3
Creditor			
Amount owed			
Monthly instalment			

4.6 Bank loans
(but excluding any mortgage previously mentioned)
(please complete for each loan)

	1	2	3
Lender			
Amount owed			
Monthly instalment			

4.7 Any other debts
(please complete for each debt)

	1	2	3
Lender			
Amount owed			
Weekly/monthly instalment			

5 MONTHLY INCOME AND EXPENDITURE

A Income

Wages or salary after tax and NI	£	per week/month
Pension	£	per week/month
Other income	£	per week/month
Partner's net wages or salary	£	per week/month
Child benefit	£	per week/month

State income (please specify)	£ .... per week/month
Maintenance	£ .... per week/month
Other (please specify)	
....	£ .... per week/month
....	£ .... per week/month
....	£ .... per week/month

B Expenditure

Mortgage or rent	£ .... per week/month
Gas/electricity	£ .... per week/month
Telephone	£ .... per week/month
Insurances (please specify)	£ .... per week/month
Pension contributions	£ .... per week/month
Travel (public transport)	£ .... per week/month
Car expenses	£ .... per week/month
Food	£ .... per week/month
Council tax	£ .... per week/month
Water rates	£ .... per week/month
Other (please specify)	£ .... per week/month
....	£ .... per week/month
....	£ .... per week/month
Total expenditure	£ .... per week/month

C Other payments

Add up any weekly/monthly instalments from
section 4 and enter the total here)   £ .... per week/month

Surplus income

Income (A)	£......... per week/month
less	
Expenditure (B+C)	£......... per week/month
Balance	£......... per week/month

Bankruptcy notice

The Public Notices section of your local newspaper will almost certainly publish bankruptcy announcements along with the applications for liquor licences and details of planning proposals. Newspaper editors often wait until they have several **bankruptcy orders** from different courts, including the High Court in London, and publish everything in one batch. Here is a fictitious ad in respect of poor Mr Micawber.

INSOLVENCY ACT 1986

IN BANKRUPTCY

Bankruptcy Orders have been made in the undermentioned courts against the following (note: all debts due to the estate should be paid to me):

IPSWICH COUNTY COURT

No. 12 of 2003 RE: WILKINS MICAWBER – Occupation Unknown, of The Debtor's Prison, otherwise known as Hansbrow's Hotel, London, and lately residing at Hope House, Optimist Close, Ipswich, Suffolk. On 8 January 2002 the above-named court made a Bankruptcy Order against Wilkins Micawber. The First meeting of Creditors will be held on 14 February 2004 at my address –

April 8 2003

Miss J Griptight, Official Receiver, 2nd Floor, Hardup House, Dickens Road, Ipswich IP1 NBG

Debtor's bankruptcy petition (Form 6.27)

Rule 6.37

Form 6.27

Debtor's Bankruptcy Petition
(Title)

(a) Insert full name, address and occupation (if any) of debtor

I
(a)_____

_____

_____

(b) Insert in full any other name(s) by which the debtor is or has been known

also known as
(b)_____

(c) Insert former address or addresses at which the debtor may have incurred debts or liabilities still unpaid or unsatisfied

[lately residing at
(c)_____

_____

(d) Insert trading name (adding "with another or others", if this is so), business address and nature of the business

[and carrying on business as (d) _____

_____

_____]

(e) Insert any former trading names (adding "with another or others", if this is so), business address and nature of the business in respect of which the debtor may have incurred debts or liabilities still unpaid or unsatisfied

[and lately carrying on business as (e) _____

_____

_____

_____]

request the court that a bankruptcy order be made against me and say as follows:-

(f) Delete as applicable

1. (f) [My centre of main interests has been][I have had an establishment] at

_____

OR

I carry on business as an insurance undertaking; a credit institution; investment undertaking providing services involving the holding of funds or securities for third parties; or a collective investment undertaking as referred to in Article 1.2 of the EC Regulation.

OR

My centre of main interests is not within a Member State

Under the EC Regulation
(i) Centre of main interests should correspond to the place where the debtor conducts the administration of his interests on a regular basis.
(ii) Establishment is defined in the Council Regulation (No 1346/2000) on insolvency proceedings as "any place of operations where the debtor caries out a non-transitory economic activity with human means and goods"

LETTERS AND FORMS

149

2. I have for the greater part of six months immediately preceding the presentation of this petition (f) [resided at] [carried on business at]_____

_____

(g) Insert name of court

within the district of (f) [this court] [(g)   county court]. I am presenting my petition to this court, as it is the nearest full-time county court to (g)   county court, for the following reasons:

(h) State reasons

(h)

3. I am unable to pay my debts.

4. (f) That within the period of five years ending with the date of this petition:-

(j) Insert date

(i) I have not been adjudged bankrupt

(k) Insert name of court

OR

(l) Insert number of bankruptcy proceedings

I was adjudged bankrupt on (j)   in the (k)

Court No. (l)

(ii) I have not (f) [made a composition with my creditors in satisfaction of my debts] or (f) [entered into a scheme of arrangement with creditors] (S16 BA1914)

OR

On (j)   I (f) [made a composition] [entered into a scheme of arrangement] with my creditors.

(iii) I have not entered into a voluntary arrangement

OR

On (j)   I entered into a voluntary arrangement

(iv) I have not been subject to an administration order under Part VI of the County Courts Act 1984

OR

On (j)   an administration order was made against me in the (l)   county court.

5. A statement of my affairs is filed with this petition.

Date_____

Signature_____

Complete only if petition not heard immediately

Endorsement
This petition having been presented to the court on _____ it is ordered that the petition shall be heard as follows:-
Date _____
Time _____ hours
Place_____

Statement of Affairs (Form 6.28)

Rule 6.41(1)

NOTE:
These details
will be the
same as those
shown at the
top of your
petition

Statement of Affairs (Debtor's Petition)   Form 6.28
Insolvency Act 1986
In the

In Bankruptcy

No. _____ of 20 _____

Re _____
The 'Guidance Notes' Booklet tells you how to complete this form easily and
correctly

Show your current financial position and supply the required information by
completing all the pages of this form, which will then be your Statement of
Affairs

_____

AFFIDAVIT

When you have completed the rest of this form, this Affidavit must be sworn
before a Solicitor or Commissioner for Oaths or an officer of the court duly
authorised to administer oaths

(a) Insert full
name and
occupation
(b) Insert full
address

I (a) _____
_____
of (b) _____
_____
_____
Make oath and say that the several pages marked
_____
and contained in the exhibit marked "Z"

are to the best of my knowledge and belief a full, true and complete statement
of my affairs at today's date.

Sworn at

Dated this _____ day of _____ 20 _____ Signature(s) _____
Before me _____

_____

A Solicitor or Commissioner for Oaths or authorised officer

Before swearing the affidavit, the Solicitor or Commissioner is particularly
requested to make sure that the full name, address and description of the
deponent are stated, and to initial any crossing out or other alterations in the
printed form. A deficiency in the affidavit in any of the above respects will
mean it will be refused by the court, and will need to be re-sworn.

IN THE   No   of 20

IN BANKRUPTCY

Re

This is the exhibit marked "Z" referred to in the annexed affidavit of

sworn on the   day of   20

Before me

Officer appointed to administer oaths

Section 1 :   **Personal Details**

1.1	Surname	
	Forename(s)	
	Title (Mr, Mrs, Ms etc)	
1.2	Any other names by which you have been known (such as maiden name, alias or nickname).	
1.3	Date of birth	
1.4	Place of birth	
1.5	National insurance number (if known)	
1.6	Home address	
1.7	Home telephone number	
1.8	Mobile telephone number	
1.9	On which telephone number can you be contacted during the day?	
1.10	E-mail address	

1.11   Are you (tick all that apply):

	Single		Co-habiting	
	Married		Separated	
	Divorced		Widowed	

1.12   Are you, or in the last 5 years have you been, involved in proceedings for divorce or separation?   **Yes** ☐   **No** ☐

1

1.13 Have you been bankrupt before?

Yes ☐   No ☐

If **Yes**, when?

Which court and which Official Receiver's office dealt with the proceedings?

1.14 Have you previously entered, or have you tried to enter, into an Individual Voluntary Arrangement (a formal arrangement with your creditors, ratified by the Court, to pay them in full or part over time)?

Yes ☐   No ☐

If **Yes**, give the name and address of the insolvency practitioner involved and the date of the arrangement.

1.15 Are you involved in any legal proceedings?

Yes ☐   No ☐

If **Yes**, please give brief details of the nature of the proceedings, the name and address of any solicitor acting for you, the name of the relevant court and any case or reference number.

1.16 Are you, or in the last five years, have you been a director or involved in the management of a company?

Yes ☐   No ☐

2

Please complete this section if you are or have been self-employed (including a partner in a partnership) at any time in the last two years. If not, go to Section 3.

2.1	What was the name of your business?		
2.2	State the type of business, trade or profession		
2.3	What was the trading address? (this should also be listed in Section 8)		
2.4	Was the business registered for VAT?	**Yes**	**No**
	If **Yes**, give the VAT number.		
2.5	If the business was a partnership give the name(s) and address(es) of the partner(s)		
2.6	When did the business start trading?		
2.7	If it has stopped trading, when did it do so?		
2.8	At what address are your books of account and other accounting records kept?		
2.9	If you hold records on a computer, provide details of which records are held and state where the computer is.		
2.10	What is the name and address of your accountant?		
2.11	What is the name and address of your solicitor?		

3

2.12 Have you employed anybody during the last two years? Yes ☐ No ☐

If **Yes**, do you owe them any money or may any former employee claim that you owe them any money, e.g. for wages, holiday pay or redundancy pay? Yes ☐ No ☐

⬇

Details of employees to whom money is or may be owing should be included in your list of creditors in Section 4.

4

Section 3 :	Assets

An asset is something that you own, either alone or jointly.

Please list everything you own, including assets of your business (if any), and their approximate amount value.

You should also mark any assets that are perishable or likely to reduce in value if not realised quickly (e.g. they are incurring fees that need to be paid before the item can be collected) with a *.

If a creditor (see section 4) has a claim over an asset, put the letter "S" against the asset in this list and mal sure the creditor is included on the 'Secured Creditors' page of section 4.

To help you, here is a list of the types of asset you may own.

- ➤ Cash in hand
- ➤ Cash in bank, building society or similar account

- ➤ Cash held by anyone for you
- ➤ Money owed to you

- ➤ Stock in trade
- ➤ Tools of trade, plant and equipment, machinery

- ➤ Fixtures and fittings
- ➤ Farming stock and crops

- ➤ Leasehold land and property
- ➤ Freehold land and property

- ➤ National Savings and Premium Bonds
- ➤ Stocks, shares and other investments

- ➤ Pension policies and other pension entitlements
- ➤ Endowment and other life policies

- ➤ Any property or sums due to you under a will or trust
- ➤ Any property abroad in which you have an interest, including timeshares

- ➤ Motor vehicles
- ➤ Any other property of any value, e.g. paintings, furniture or jewellery

Remember

You must take or send any documents relating to your assets to the Official Receiver. These may include su things such as documents of title, share certificates, investments, life assurance documents, and pension policies.

If you do not disclose all of your assets, you may commit a criminal offence.

5

Section 3 cont:	List of Assets

3.1	Details	Approximate value £
1.		
2.		
3.		
4.		
5.		
6.		
7.		
8.		
9.		
10.		

6

PERSONAL INSOLVENCY

	Details	Approximate value £
11.		
12.		
13.		
14.		
15.		
16.		
17.		
18.		
19.		
20.		

7

3.2   Have you in the last five years given away, transferred or sold for less than its true value any property or possessions you owned? This includes the surrender of life, endowment and pension policies.   **Yes** ☐   **No** ☐

If **Yes**, please provide the following details.

Description of the asset	When did you give away, transfer or sell the asset?	Name and address of recipient	Estimated market value or true value of the asset	Value at which the asset was given away, transferred or sold

3.3   Do you own a motor vehicle or have you disposed of any vehicle in the last 6 months? (if you own a motor vehicle, this should also be listed in Q3.1)   **Yes** ☐   **No** ☐

If **Yes**, please provide the following details:

Make	
Registration number	
Estimated value £	
Finance outstanding £	
Location of vehicle	
Name of any joint owner	

3.4   If you have disposed of any vehicle in the last 6 months, please specify where the vehicle is now.

8

Section 3 cont:	Assets

3.5   Do you have the use of a motor vehicle that you do not own?

Yes [ ]   No [ ]

If **Yes**, please provide the following details:

Registration number	
Owner	
Estimated value £	

3.6   Has an enforcement officer (previously known as sheriff's officer) / bailiff visited you in the last 6 months?

Yes [ ]   No [ ]

(An enforcement officer / bailiff is an officer of the court who may attend to remove assets for sale, if, for example, a judgment debt has not been paid)

If **Yes**, please provide the following details:

Name of creditor	Amount of claim £	Date distress levied	Description and estimated value of property seized

9

Creditors are people to whom you owe money.

Complete the lists on the next few pages, giving full names and postal addresses of everyone to whom you owe money, including any account, agreement or reference numbers where known.

The first page is for secured creditors, i.e. creditors who have a claim over something of yours, such as a mortgage or charge over your home. The amounts owing to these creditors should show only the net debt (the amount owing after taking off the value of the asset concerned).If the asset is worth more than the amount of the debt, put 'Nil' in the 'Net amount owing' column. You should include any property or goods that are covered by hire purchase agreements in this section.

The remaining pages of this section are for unsecured creditors, i.e. those who do not have a claim over anything of yours.

Where the debt or amount is in dispute, write the amount being claimed by the creditor in the 'Amount owing' column and also the amount you think you owe. Mark the disputed debts with the letter "D".

If any of the debts are owed as a result of being a member of a partnership, mark them with the letter "P".

If any of the debts are owed to your employee(s), mark them with the letter "E".

To help you, here is a list of the types of things for which, or people to whom, you may owe money. This list is not exhaustive.

➢ Electricity	➢ Gas
➢ Rent	➢ Telephone
➢ Water rates and sewerage charges	➢ Council tax, general rates and community charge
➢ Inland Revenue	➢ Any banks or financial companies
➢ Goods or services you have received	➢ H M Customs and Excise
➢ Guarantees you have given	➢ Department for Work and Pensions
➢ Money owed to employees	➢ Leasing agreements
➢ Customers who have paid money for goods and services that you have not supplied	➢ Creditors claiming their own goods are in your possession

Remember
If the telephone, gas or electric accounts are in your name and you become bankrupt, supplies could be cut off. Contact the supply companies to arrange for any future supply you want.

10

Section 4 cont:

List of Secured Creditors
(e.g. anyone holding a mortgage or charge over property belonging to you)

Name of creditor	Address	Account, reference or agreement number (if known)	Amount owing (A) £	What of yours is claimed and what is its present value? (B) £	Net amount owing (A-B) £
				TOTAL £	

Section 4 cont: **List of Unsecured Creditors**

Name of creditor	Address	Account, reference or agreement number (if known)	Amount owing £	Date incurred	What was the debt for?
			TOTAL £		

Section 4 cont: **List of Unsecured Creditors**

Name of creditor	Address	Account, reference or agreement number (if known)	Amount owing £	Date incurred	What was the debt for?
		TOTAL £			

Note: Include any current liability also shown in Section 4.

5.1 Do you now, or have you in the last 2 years had, any
     cheque cards, cash dispenser cards, credit or charge
     cards, debit cards, etc?

Yes	No
☐	☐

5.2 If **Yes**, provide details.

Type of card	Card number	Name and address of bank or supplier	Date obtained

5.3 Are any of the above accounts or cards
     held jointly with anyone else?

Yes	No
☐	☐

If **Yes**, provide details

WARNING:
If you become bankrupt, you must not use any cheques, cheque cards, cash dispenser cards, credit cards, debit cards, charge cards or pass books in your possession. If you do so, you may be committing a criminal offence. You must take or send all cards (which should be cut in half), cheque books and pass books to the Official Receiver.

14

Note: Include details of accounts with a debit (overdrawn) balance also shown in Section 4.

5.4 Please list any bank, building society or National Savings accounts you hold, or have held in the last two
years, including any joint, business or dormant accounts.

Name and address (including postcodes) of banks etc	Account number	Tick if your regular income is paid into this account	Name of joint account-holder (if applicable)	Balance of account £

15

Section 6 :	Employment and Present Income

The court can order that you pay part of your earnings or other income to your trustee if your income is more than you need to live on. The order is known as an Income Payments Order and is made under section 310 of the Insolvency Act 1986. Alternatively you can enter into a voluntary arrangement with the Official Receiver or trustee called an Income Payments Agreement under section 310A of the Insolvency Act 1986.

You must answer the following questions about your income and outgoings and you may be asked to provide your wage slips or salary statements and bills such as gas or electricity to support your answers. This will enable a decision to be made as to whether an Income Payments Order or an Income Payments Agreement is appropriate.

The court will not make an Income Payments Order, neither would an Income Payments Agreement be agreed, that would leave you too little income to meet the reasonable domestic needs of you and your family.

If an Income Payments Order or an Income Payments Agreement is made against you, the payments will usually stop after 3 years.

If your income increases while you are bankrupt, you must inform your trustee of the increase within 21 days.

6.1 Are you: employed ☐   self-employed ☐   unemployed ☐

If you are unemployed, when did you last work?

6.2 If employed, what is your job and who is your employer? What is the address of the personnel department and your pay reference number?
When did you start this job?

If self-employed, give the name and address of the business.

6.3 What is your average monthly take-home pay (include, for example, overtime, commission and bonuses).

£

6.4 How much tax do you usually pay each month?

£

16

PERSONAL INSOLVENCY

6.5 How much do you pay in National Insurance
     each month?

£

6.6 Do you receive any other income,
     including state benefits or tax credits?   Yes   No

     If **Yes**, state from what source (for
     example pension, state benefits, part-time
     earnings) and how much you receive
     each month?

£

6.7 How much do other members of your
     household contribute each month to
     the household expenses?

£

6.8 Total household income
     (Q6.3 + 6.6 + 6.7)

£

6.9 Give your current (or last)
     Income Tax reference number.

     Address of tax office
     (including postcode)

17

6.10 Do you have any current attachment of earnings orders in force
      against you?   **Yes** ☐   **No** ☐

If **Yes**, give details

Name of creditor	Date of first payment	Date last payment due	Court	Amount of each payment and whether monthly or weekly £	Total amount paid to date £

18

The information in this section may be used to work out how much, if anything, you can afford to pay your creditors each month. It is important that it is accurate and that you include all necessary expenditure.

7.1 How much do you spend each month on the following:-

Mortgage payments or rent on your home   £

Housekeeping (including food and cleaning)   £

Gas, electricity, other heating   £

Water   £

Telephone charges   £

Travelling to and from work and other essential journeys   £

Clothing   £

Maintenance payments and fines   £

Council tax   £

Other essential payments (e.g. life/household insurance, **payments** car tax & repairs)   £   ➤ **Provide details of these**

Total   £

19

Section 8:

Current Property
(including properties used for residential and business purposes)

8.1 Give details of any properties you own. (these should also be listed in Q3.1)

Address, type of property (e.g. flat, semi-detached house), number of bedrooms and whether freehold or leasehold	Approximate value of property (A) £	Name and address(es) of any joint owner(s)	Name and address of anyone who holds a charge or mortgage over your property.	Amount owing to each secured creditor (B) £	Net value of the property (A)-(B) £

8.2 Give details of any properties you rent or lease, either alone or jointly.

Address of property	Monthly rent £	Name and address(es) of any joint tenant(s)	Name and address of landlord

You must take or send to the Official Receiver a copy of your lease or rent agreement. A rent demand or rent book will help if you do not have a copy agreement.

20

PERSONAL INSOLVENCY

Section 8 cont: **Current Property**

8.3 Apart from properties that you own, rent or lease, are there any other properties in which you may otherwise have an interest?

Yes ☐   No ☐

If **Yes**, give details

Address of property, type of property (e.g. flat, semi-terraced) and number of bedrooms	Who lets you use it?	How much do you pay?	Is there a written agreement?

8.4 Does anyone else have interest in any of the properties that you own, rent or lease? This interest may be as a sub-tenant, a guarantor of the mortgage, a partner, a joint tenant, joint lessee or otherwise.

Yes ☐   No ☐

If **Yes**, give details

Address of property (including postcode)	Name of person with an interest	Their address, if different from the property (including postcode) and reference	Nature of interest

Section 9 :	Property Disposed of in the last Five Years				

9.1 Give details of any properties, owned alone or jointly, that you have sold, given away or transferred in the five years before the presenting of your bankruptcy petition.

Address of property	Value of property £	When did you sell, transfer or give away the property?	To whom did you sell, transfer or give away the property?	Net sale proceeds (less any charges and legal fees) £

22

10.1 Give the names and ages of all
      occupants of your household and
      state which, if any, are dependent
      on you.

10.2 Apart from members of your household,
      is any other person dependent upon you?

                                              Yes   No

      If **Yes**, provide details including
      their name, address and reason
      for dependency

23

11.1   When did you first have difficulty paying your debts?

11.2   What do you think are the reasons for you not having enough money to pay your debts? You should provide reasons to support your answer. For example, it would not be enough to state "the recession" without explaining its effect on your affairs.

11.3   Have you lost any money through betting or gambling during the last two years?   **Yes**

   No

If **Yes**, how much have you lost?

24

Section 12 :	**Declaration**

I hereby confirm that my answers to all the above questions (including any extra information on pages following this declaration) are to the best of my knowledge and belief a true and accurate statement of my affairs as at today's date. I understand that I may be committing a criminal offence if I deliberately give false information in relation to my bankruptcy.

Your signature

Name in BLOCK CAPITALS

Date

25

Question
the
   No:
column.

If there is insufficient space on any page, you should continue your answer to

question on this page. The question number should be given in the left-hand

26

PERSONAL INSOLVENCY

Section 13 cont:	Extra Information

Question
No:

27

Statutory demand (no judgment debt) (Form 6.1)

Rule 6.1

Statutory Demand under section 268(1)(a) of the Insolvency Act 1986. Debt for Liquidated Sum Payable Immediately

Notes for Creditor

- If the creditor is entitled to the debt by way of assignment, details of the original creditor and any intermediary assignees should be given in part C on page 3.
- If the amount of debt includes interest not previously notified to the debtor as included in the debtor's liability, details should be given, including the grounds upon which interest is charged. The amount of interest must be shown separately.
- Any other charge accruing due from time to time may be claimed. The amount or rate of the charge must be identified and the grounds on which it is claimed must be stated.
- In either case the amount claimed must be limited to that which has accrued due at the date of the demand.
- If the creditor holds any security the amount of the debt should be the sum the creditor is prepared to regard as unsecured for the purposes of this demand. Brief details of the total debt should be included and the nature of the security and the value put upon it by the creditor, as at the date of the demand, must be specified.
- If signatory of the demand is a solicitor or other agent of the creditor the name of his/her firm should be given.

*Delete if signed by the creditor himself

Warning

- This is an **important** document. You should refer to the notes entitled "How to comply with a statutory demand or have it set aside".
- If you wish to have this demand set aside you must make application to do so **within 18 days** from its service on you.
- If you do not apply to set aside **within 18 days** or otherwise deal with this demand as set out in the notes **within 21 days** after its service on you, you could be made bankrupt and your property and goods taken away from you.
- Please read the demand and notes carefully. If you are in any doubt about your position you should seek advice **immediately** from a solicitor, a Citizen Advice Bureau, or a licensed insolvency practitioner.

Demand

To _____

Address _____

_____

This demand is served on you by the creditor:

Name _____

Address _____

The creditor claims that you owe the sum of £_____, full particulars of which are set out on page 2, and that it is payable immediately and, to the extent of the sum demanded, is unsecured.

The creditor demands that you pay the above debt or secure or compound for it to the creditor's satisfaction.

[The creditor making this demand is a Minister of the Crown or a Government Department, and it is intended to present a bankruptcy petition in the High Court.]

Signature of individual _____

Name _____
(BLOCK LETTERS)

Date _____

*Position with or relationship to creditor _____

*I am authorised to make this demand on the creditor's behalf.

Address _____

_____

Tel. No. _____ Ref. _____

N.B. The person making this demand must complete the whole of pages 1, 2 and parts A, B and C (as applicable) on page 3.

Particulars of Debt
(These particulars must include (a) when the debt was incurred, (b) the consideration for the debt (or if there is no consideration the way in which it arose) and (c) the amount due as at the date of this demand.)

Notes for Creditor
Please make sure that you have read the notes on page 1 before completing this page.

Note:
If space is insufficient continue on page 4 and clearly indicate on this page that you are doing so.

Part A
Appropriate Court for Setting Aside Demand

Rule 6.4(2) of the Insolvency Rules 1986 states that the appropriate court is the court to which you would have to present your own bankruptcy petition in accordance with Rule 6.40(1) and 6.40(2). In accordance with those rules on present information the appropriate court is [the High Court of Justice]
[·   County Court]
(address)

Any application by you to set aside this demand should be made to that court.

Part B

The individual or individuals to whom any communication regarding this demand may be addressed is / are:

Name

    (BLOCK LETTERS)

Address

Telephone
Number_____

Reference

Part C
For completion if the creditor is entitled to the debt by way of assignment

	Name	Date(s) of Assignment
Original creditor		
Assignees		

How to comply with a statutory demand or have it set aside (ACT WITHIN 18 DAYS)

If you wish to avoid a bankruptcy petition being presented against you, you must pay the debt shown on page 1, particulars of which are set out on page 2 of this notice, within the period of **21 days** after its service upon you. Alternatively, you can attempt to come to a settlement with the creditor. To do this you should:

- inform the individual (or one of the individuals) named in part B above immediately that you are willing and able to offer security for the debt to the creditor's satisfaction; or

- inform the individual (or one of the individuals) named in part B immediately that you are willing and able to compound for the debt to the creditor's satisfaction.

If you dispute the demand in whole or in part you should:

- contact the individual (or one of the individuals) named in part B immediately.

THERE ARE MORE IMPORTANT NOTES ON THE NEXT PAGE

If you consider that you have grounds to have this demand set aside or if you do not quickly receive a satisfactory written reply from the individual named in part B whom you have contacted you should **apply within 18 days** from the date of service of this demand on you to the appropriate court shown in part A above to have the demand set aside.

Any application to set aside the demand (Form 6.4 in Schedule 4 to the Insolvency Rules 1986) should be made within 18 days from the date of service upon you and be supported by an affidavit (Form 6.5 in Schedule 4 to those Rules) stating the grounds on which the demand should be set aside. The forms may be obtained from the appropriate court when you attend to make the application.

Remember! – From the date of service on you of this document
    (a) you have only 18 days to apply to the court to have the demand set aside, and
    (b) you have only 21 days before the creditor may present a bankruptcy petition

Statutory demand (where there is already a judgment debt) (Form 6.2)

Rule 6.7

Form 6.2

Statutory Demand under section 268(1)(a) of the Insolvency Act 1986. Debt for Liquidated Sum Payable Immediately Following a Judgment or Order of the Court

Notes for Creditor

- If the Creditor is entitled to the debt by way of assignment, details of the original creditor and any intermediary assignees should be given in part C on page 3.

- If the amount of debt includes interest not previously notified to the debtor as included in the debtor's liability, details should be given, including the grounds upon which interest is charged. The amount of interest must be shown separately.

- Any other charge accruing due from time to time may be claimed. The amount or rate of the charge must be identified and the grounds on which it is claimed must be stated.

- In either case the amount claimed must be limited to that which has accrued due at the date of the demand.

- If the creditor holds any security the amount of debt should be the sum the creditor is prepared to regard as unsecured for the purposes of this demand. Brief details of the total debt should be included and the nature of the security and the value put upon it by the creditor, as at the date of the demand, must be specified.

- Details of the judgment or order should be inserted, including details of the Division of the Court or District Registry and court reference, where judgment is obtained in the High Court.

- If signatory of the demand is a solicitor or other agent of the creditor the name of his/her firm should be given.

*Delete if signed by the creditor himself.

Warning

- This is an **important** document. You should refer to the notes entitled "How to comply with a statutory demand or have it set aside".

- If you wish to have this demand set aside you must make application to do so **within 18 days** from its service on you.

- If you do not apply to set aside **within 18 days** or otherwise deal with this demand as set out in the notes **within 21 days** after its service on you, you could be made bankrupt and your property and goods taken away from you.

- Please read the demand and notes carefully. If you are in any doubt about your position you should seek advice **immediately** from a solicitor or your nearest Citizens Advice Bureau.

DEMAND

To

Address

This demand is served on you by the creditor:

Name

Address

The creditor claims that you owe the sum of £
full particulars of which are set out on page 2, and that it is payable immediately and, to the extent of the sum demanded, is unsecured.
By a Judgment/Order of the   court in proceedings entitled Case
Number   between
Plaintiff and
Defendant it was adjudged/ordered that you pay to the creditor the sum of £
and £   for costs.

The creditor demands that you do pay the above debt or secure or compound for it to the creditor's satisfaction.

[The creditor making this demand is a Minister of the Crown or a Government Department, and it is intended to present a bankruptcy petition in the High Court in London.]
[Delete if inappropriate]

Signature of individual
Name
(BLOCK LETTERS)

Date

*Position with or relationship to creditor

*I am authorised to make this demand on the creditor's behalf.
Address

Tel No   Ref.

N.B. The person making this demand must complete the whole of pages 1, 2 and parts A, B and C (as applicable) on page 3.

Particulars of Debt
(These particulars must include (a) when the debt was incurred, (b) the consideration for the debt (or if is there is no consideration the way in which it arose) and (c) the amount due as at the date of this demand).

Notes for Creditor
Please make sure that you have read the notes on page 1 before completing this page.

Note:
If space is insufficient continue on page 4 and clearly indicate on this page that you are doing so.

6.2 Statutory Demand under section 268(1)(a) of the Insolvency Act 1986. Debt for Liquidated Sum Payable Immediately Following a Judgment or Order of the Court 11/99

PERSONAL INSOLVENCY

Part A

Appropriate Court for Setting Aside Demand

Rule 6.4(2) of the Insolvency Rules 1986 states that the appropriate court is the court to which you would have to present your own bankruptcy petition in accordance with Rule 6.40(1) and 6.40(2).

Any application by you to set aside this demand should be made to that court, or , if this demand is issued by a Minister of the Crown or a Government Department, you must apply to the High Court to set aside if it is intended to present a bankruptcy petition against you in the High Court (see page 1).

In accordance with those rules on present information the appropriate court is [the High Court of Justice].
[County Court]
(address)

Part B

The individual or individuals to whom any communication regarding this demand may be addressed is/are:

Name _____
(BLOCK LETTERS)
Address _____

Telephone Number _____

Reference _____

Part C

For completion if the creditor is entitled to the debt by way of assignment

	Name	Date(s) of Assignment
Original creditor		
Assignees		

THERE ARE IMPORTANT NOTES ON THE NEXT PAGE

6.2 Statutory Demand under section 268(1)(a) of the Insolvency Act 1986. Debt for Liquidated Sum Payable Immediately Following a Judgment or Order of the Court 11/99

LETTERS AND FORMS

How to comply with a statutory demand or have it set aside (ACT WITHIN 18 DAYS)

If you wish to avoid a bankruptcy petition being presented against you, you must pay the debt shown on page 1, particulars of which are set out on page 2 of this notice, within the period of **21 days** after its service upon you. However, if the demand follows (includes) a judgment or order of a County Court, any payment must be made to that County Court (quoting the Case No.). Alternatively, you can attempt to come to a settlement with the creditor. To do this you should:

- inform the individual (or one of the individuals) named in part B above immediately that you are willing and able to offer security for the debt to the creditor's satisfaction; or

- inform the individual (or one of the individuals) named in part B immediately that you are willing and able to compound for the debt to the creditor's satisfaction.

If you dispute the demand in whole or in part you should:

- contact the individual (or one of the individuals) named in part B immediately.

If you consider that you have grounds to have this demand set aside or if you do not quickly receive a satisfactory written reply from the individual named in part B whom you have contacted you should **apply within 18 days** from the date of service of this demand on you to the appropriate court shown in part A above to have the demand set aside.

Any application to set aside the demand (Form 6.4 in Schedule 4 to the Insolvency Rules 1986) should be made within 18 days from the date of service upon you and be supported by an affidavit (Form 6.5 in Schedule 4 to those Rules) stating the grounds on which the demand should be set aside. The forms may be obtained from the appropriate court when you attend to make the application.

REMEMBER!—	From the date of service on you of this document (a) you have only 18 days to apply to the court to have the demand set aside, and (b) you have only 21 days before the creditor may present a bankruptcy petition

6.2 Statutory Demand under section 268(1)(a) of the Insolvency Act 1986. Debt for Liquidated Sum Payable Immediately Following a Judgment or Order of the Court 11/99

PERSONAL INSOLVENCY

Rule 6.6

Form 6.7

**Creditor's Bankruptcy Petition on Failure to Comply with a
Statutory Demand for a Liquidated Sum Payable Immediately
(Title)**

(a) Insert full names(s) and address(es) of petitioner(s)

I/We (a)_____

(b) Insert full name, place of residence and occupation (if any) of debtor

_____

_____

petition the court that a bankruptcy order may be made against (b)_____

_____

(c) Insert in full any other name(s) by which the debtor is or has been known

[also known as (c)_____]

(d) Insert trading name (adding "with another or others", if this is so), business address and nature of business

[and carrying on business as (d)_____

_____]

(e) Insert any other address or addresses at which the debtor has resided at or after the time the petition debt was incurred

[and lately residing at (e)_____

_____]

(f) Give the same details as specified in note (d) above for any other businesses which have been carried on at or after the time the petition debt was incurred

[and lately carrying on business as (f)_____

_____]

and say as follows:-

(g) Delete as applicable

1. (g) [The debtor's centre of main interests has been][The debtor has had an establishment] at _____

OR

The debtor carries on business as an insurance undertaking; a credit institution; an investment undertaking providing services involving the holding of funds or securities for third parties; or a collective investment undertaking as referred to in Article 1.2 of the EC Regulation

OR

The debtor's centre of main interests is not within a Member State

2. The debtor has for the greater part of six months immediately preceding the presentation of this petition (g) [resided at] [carried on business at]

(h) Or as the case may be following the terms of Rule 6.9

_____

within the district of this court (h)

Under the EC Regulation:
(i) The centre of main interests should correspond to the place where the debtor conducts the administration of his interests on a regular basis.
(ii) Establishment is defined as "any place of operations where the debtor caries out a non-transitory economic activity with human means and goods".

2. I have for the greater part of six months immediately preceding the presentation of this petition (f) [resided at] [carried on business at]_____

(g) Insert name of court

within the district of (f) [this court] [(g)   county court]. I am presenting my petition to this court, as it is the nearest full-time county court to (g)   county court, for the following reasons:

(h) State reasons

(h)

3. I am unable to pay my debts.

4. (f) That within the period of five years ending with the date of this petition:-

(j) Insert date

(i) I have not been adjudged bankrupt

(k) Insert name of court

OR

(l) Insert number of bankruptcy proceedings

I was adjudged bankrupt on (j)   in the (k)

Court No. (l)

(ii) I have not (f) [made a composition with my creditors in satisfaction of my debts] or (f) [entered into a scheme of arrangement with creditors] (S16 BA1914)

OR

On (j)   I (f) [made a composition] [entered into a scheme of arrangement] with my creditors.

(iii) I have not entered into a voluntary arrangement

OR

On (j)   I entered into a voluntary arrangement

(iv) I have not been subject to an administration order under Part VI of the County Courts Act 1984

OR

On (j)   an administration order was made against me in the (l)   county court.

5. A statement of my affairs is filed with this petition.

Date_____

Signature_____

Complete only if petition not heard immediately

Endorsement

This petition having been presented to the court on _____ it is ordered that the petition shall be heard as follows:-

Date _____

Time _____ hours

Place_____

PERSONAL INSOLVENCY

Useful contacts

Department of Trade and Industry (DTI)

www.dti.gov.uk

There is much free information on this site, which also links with The Insolvency Service.

The Insolvency Service

The Insolvency Service is a section of the DTI and its useful website contains details of all the various receivers and government bodies dealing with insolvency. The home page provides links to useful articles on all aspects of individual and corporate insolvency, as well as links with many professional bodies, some of which we also review below.

The Insolvency Service Central Enquiry Line
Tel: 020 7291 6895

Email: Central.Enquiryline@insolvency.gsi.gov.uk

Publications Order Line – for copies of useful leaflets, especially *Guide to Bankruptcy*, tel: 0121 698 4241, or write to:

The Insolvency Service
(Publications Orders)
Records Management
4th Floor East
Ladywood House
Birmingham
B2 4UZ

Most of their advice leaflets are also available online: www.insolvency.gov.uk

Bankruptcy Advisory Service

Helpline: 01482 633 035

We can't find a website, although several sites recommend this organisation. You have to subscribe; it costs £15 a year.

HM Customs & Excise (VAT)

Just to prove the VAT man has a heart after all, HMCE run the National Insolvency Unit: www.hmce.gov.uk (linked with the Insolvency Service, above). They offer free guidance leaflets as well as a telephone helpdesk, manned 8.30 am to 5 pm Monday to Thursday and 8.30 am to 4 pm Friday:

Tel: 0151 703 8450.

Fax: 0151 703 8735

There is a direct email link on the website at www.hmce.gov.uk/business/services/nat-ins-unit.htm – just click on 'Insolvency Helpdesk'.

Professional bodies

Many professional bodies' websites are linked to the Insolvency Service website. Here's a selection:

Association of Business Recovery Professionals

(R3 online)

www.r3.org.uk

Most insolvency practitioners are members of their own trade organisation, the Association of Business Recovery Professionals, who have a website giving basic insolvency information and details of how to make a complaint. Don't be put off by their name; they are concerned with personal as well as business insolvency.

Insolvency Practitioners' Association

52–54 Gracechurch St
London
EC3V 0EH

Tel: 020 7623 5108
Fax: 020 7623 5127

Email: secretariat@insolvency-practitioners.org.uk
www.ipa.uk.com

This provides useful free information as well as links with several other related sites.

Checking creditworthiness

The Register of County Court Judgments

The Register is maintained by:

Registry Trust Limited
173/175 Cleveland Street
London W1T 6QR
Tel: 020 7380 0133

For £4.50 a name (make out the cheque to Registry Trust Limited) you can get a printout of any judgments against that name.

The Individual Insolvency Register

This came into operation in March 1999 and keeps details of **bankruptcy** and **individual voluntary arrangements** (**IVAs**)(a sort of halfway house between solvency and insolvency). You can apply free of charge:

o   in person at any Official Receiver's office (listed in your local telephone directory), where you fill in a form and receive a printout of the information;

o   in writing to:
      The Insolvency Service
      Bankruptcy Public Search Room
      4th Floor, East Wing
      45–46 Stephenson Street
      Birmingham B2 4UZ

o   by telephone to the Insolvency Service: 020 7637 1110, and they will tell you over the phone whether an individual is bankrupt (or is subject to bankruptcy proceedings) or has entered into an IVA.

Business Debt Line

Tel: 0800 197 6026 Monday–Friday 10 am–4 pm, plus 24 hour answering machine service.

This is a free telephone debt counselling service for the self-employed and small businesses facing insolvency. Advice is independent and confidential.

Community Legal Service

Run by the Legal Services Commission, formerly the Legal Aid Board. Solicitors who participate in their scheme can give free legal advice if you qualify. Call 0845 608 1122 for a solicitor near you, or access the website: www.justask.org.uk

They have also launched a debtline, tel 0845 1232 321, lines open 8 am–6 pm (charged at local rate).

National Debt Line

Free, confidential and independent advice over the telephone; self-help information pack also available.

Tel: 0808 808 4000 Monday–Friday 9 am to 9 pm, Saturday 9.30 am to 1 pm; plus 24 hour answering machine service.

www.nationaldebtline.co.uk

Consumer Credit Counselling Service

Tel: 0800 138 1111

Another useful free helpline.

Business Link

www.businesslink.gov.uk

This government agency helps small businesses and provides them with high quality information.

Tel: 08456 009 006

Call a CAB

www.nacab.org.uk or www.adviceguide.org.uk

The National Association of Citizens Advice Bureaux (CAB) website offers general advice on debt as well as details of CAB offices near you. From the home page, click on Consumer and Debt.

Or check your local telephone directory for a CAB near you.

Credit to Cash

www.credit-to-cash.com

'Credit to Cash is registered by the Office of Fair Trading to counsel debtors'. This website offers much free advice on everything from starting up a business to advice on debt. We cannot positively recommend this site, as we haven't studied everything in detail, but there is certainly a lot of free information there, together with the offer of a free consultation with an insolvency professional near you.

British Bankers' Association

This Association publishes a leaflet called *Dealing with Debt – How your bank can help*, available online at www.bba.org.uk/pdf/dealingwithdebt03.pdf.

Sadly, it does not list banks who offer services to bankrupts.

Inland Revenue

www.inlandrevenue.gov.uk

The BBC

BBC Watchdog reports

A wealth of useful information about money matters: key in www.bbc.co.uk/watchdog

Other useful BBC sites

http://news.bbc.co.uk/1/hi/programmes/moneybox

http://news.bbc.co.uk/1/hi/business/your_money

Credit Reference Agencies

Equifax plc
Credit File Advice Centre
PO Box 1140
Bradford
BD1 5US

www.equifax.co.uk

Experian Ltd
Consumer Help
PO Box 8000
Nottingham
NG1 5GX

www.experian.co.uk

Callcredit plc
PO Box 491
Leeds
LS3 1WZ

www.callcredit.plc.uk

More helplines and websites

www.ukcreditrepair.co.uk

A wealth of advice on credit repair, including avoiding the cowboys!

CIFAS (fraud prevention)

Protective Registration Team, care of Equifax

Tel: 08700 102 091

CIFAS
PO Box 1141
Bradford BD1 5UR

The Information Commissioner

Free booklet *No Credit?* from the Information Commissioner. Just call 01625 545700 and ask for your free copy or write to:

Information Commissioner's Office
Wycliffe House
Water Lane
Wilmslow
Cheshire SK9 5AF

And finally ... The Three Wise Men!

Frank Brumby
Leathes Prior Solicitors
74 The Close
Norwich
Norfolk NR1 4DR

Tel: 01603 610911

Their website:
www.leathesprior.co.uk
even has a mug shot of Frank ...

Chris Williams and Andrew McTear
McTear Williams & Wood
90 St Faiths Lane
Norwich NR1 1NE

Tel: 01603 877540
Fax: 01603 877549

Index

Notes

Notes

Notes

Notes

Notes

Notes

Notes

Notes

Notes

Notes

Notes